Contents

Introduction

About the series
Why choose this depth study?
Aims of *The USA between the Wars 1919–1941*
Structure
Organising your course
Using the material in the classroom
Learning trouble spots
Coursework

Detailed teachers' notes

Section 1: Was the USA the land of opportunity?
Section 2: The USA in the 1920s: Was this a good time for all?
Section 3: Crash and Depression
Section 4: Did Roosevelt save America?

Photocopiable worksheets

1	Coming to America
2	Map of the USA
3	The government of the USA
4	Two Republican Presidents
5	How could you become the President?
6	The boom in the 1920s
7	What were the main features of the boom?
8	The causes of the boom in the 1920s
9	Why was there a boom in the USA in the 1920s?
10A–B	Would you have made a good Republican president in the 1920s?
11	Would you have wanted to work for Henry Ford?
12	The significance of Henry Ford
13	Why is Henry Ford significant in American history?
14	Who didn't benefit from the boom?
15	The Red Scare
16	Rough justice for Sacco and Vanzetti
17	The Ku Klux Klan
18	The Rosewood incident
19	Two black leaders
20	Religious revival in the 1920s
21	Will you vote for Prohibition?
22	Why did Prohibition fail?
23	Gangsters
24	What were the causes of the Wall Street Crash?
25	Black people in the Depression
26	Why did Roosevelt win the 1932 election?
27	The New Deal in action
28	Criticising the New Deal
29	Opponents of the New Deal
30	Assessing the New Deal
31	Two views of the NRA
32	How successful was the New Deal?
33	An obituary for Franklin D. Roosevelt

SHP provision for GCSE

Depth Studies

- Germany 1919–1945   Students' Book   01795 7059 X
                                        Teachers' Book   01795 7220 7

- Russia & the USSR 1905–1941   Students' Book   01795 5255 9
                                        Teachers' Book   01795 5256 7

- The USA between the Wars 1919-1941   Students' Book   01795 5259 1
                                        Teachers' Book   01795 5260 5

- The American West   Students' Book   01795 5181 1
                                        Teachers' Book   01795 5182 X

- Britain & the Great War   Students' Book   01795 7347 5
                                        Teachers' Book   01795 7348 3

Development Studies

- Crime & Punishment through Time   Students' Book   01795 5261 3
                                        Teachers' Book   01795 5262 1

- Medicine & Health through Time   Students' Book   01795 5265 6
                                        Teachers' Book   01795 5266 4

DISCOVERING THE PAST FOR GCSE

Terry Fiehn
Rik Mills
Maggie Samuelson
Carol White

Series Editor:
Colin Shephard

THE USA BETWEEN THE WARS 1919–1941

TEACHERS' RESOURCE BOOK

JOHN MURRAY

Acknowledgements

p.44 Brown Brothers.

Every effort has been made to trace copyright holders, and the publishers apologise for any omissions, which they will be pleased to rectify at the earliest opportunity.

Special thanks to Jack Fiehn for researching material for this book and writing the sections on black Americans.

Note: The wording and sentence structure of some written sources have been adapted and simplified to make them accessible to all students, while faithfully preserving the sense of the original.

Series consultants
Terry Fiehn
Tim Lomas
Martin and Jenny Tucker

© Terry Fiehn, Rik Mills, Maggie Samuelson, Carol White 1998

First published in 1998
by John Murray (Publishers) Ltd
50 Albemarle Street
London W1S 4BD

Reprinted 2001, 2002

All rights reserved. The material in this publication is copyright but permission is given to teachers to make copies of the worksheets for one-time use as instructional material within their own school (or other educational institution). This permission does not extend to the making of copies for use outside the institution in which they are made (e.g. in a resource centre), and the material may not be copied in unlimited quantities, kept on behalf of others, passed on or sold to third parties, or stored for future use in a retrieval system. If you wish to use the material in any way other than as specified you must apply in writing to the publishers.

Layouts by Colour House, Luton
Illustrations by Peter Glazier
Typeset in $10\frac{1}{2}/12$ pt Walbaum Book by
Colour House, Luton, Bedfordshire
Printed in Great Britain by Selwood Printing Ltd., Burgess Hill, West Sussex
A CIP catalogue record for this book is available from the British Library

ISBN 0 7195 5260 5
Students' Book ISBN 0 7195 5259 1

INTRODUCTION

About the series

Discovering the Past
Series Editor: Colin Shephard

Discovering the Past for GCSE
Discovering the Past is the Schools History Project's series of course books for Key Stage 3 and GCSE.

At GCSE level *Discovering the Past* resources both SHP GCSE syllabuses and Modern World History. A full list of titles in the GCSE series can be found on the page opposite.

Coherence across the key stages
Discovering the Past has become the most widely used history course at Key Stage 3. It has greatly affected teaching methods in Y7–Y9 through its core text books, option units, Special Needs Support Material, and INSET support for all aspects of history teaching and learning. *Discovering the Past for GCSE* deliberately follows many of the precedents of the Key Stage 3 books and allows users of the Key Stage 3 books to continue with similar teaching approaches.

Exam requirements
At the same time the series has adapted those techniques to suit the requirements of exam preparation. The series has been conceived, written and edited by individuals who are closely involved in GCSE examining as chief examiners, assistant examiners and moderators. The needs of students to revise content effectively, to develop their skills in extended writing, to complete coursework assignments, to express themselves effectively have been an integral part of the planning and writing of the books in the series.

Key features

■ **An issue-based approach**
Issues and questions raised by the content give each unit its identity. These genuine historical issues and controversies encourage students to question conventional interpretations of the past.

■ **The role of the individual**
By focusing on case studies of particular places and individuals, the series avoids historical stereotypes. Instead, students can begin to appreciate the variety and complexity of a period.

■ **Classroom appeal**
The series uses the best classroom practices, combining innovation and familiar techniques to ensure variety for the student and the teacher. A range of readers, advisers and the trialling schools have ensured the classroom appeal of the material across the Key Stages.

■ **Source-based learning**
The student tasks and enquiries use a wide range of source material – so that source-based work is thoroughly integrated into work on historical understanding.

■ **Enquiry and communication**
The series offers a wide range of exercises that allow students to present their historical findings in extended writing, using a variety of techniques such as reports, essays, diaries, leaflets, letters or articles.

THE SCHOOLS HISTORY PROJECT

This project was set up by the Schools Council in 1972. Its main aim was to suggest suitable objectives for history teachers, and to promote the use of appropriate materials and teaching methods for their realisation. This involved a reconsideration of the nature of history and its relevance in secondary schools, the design of a syllabus framework which shows the uses of history in the teaching of adolescents, and the setting up of appropriate examinations.

Since 1978 the project has been based at Trinity and All Saints' College, Leeds. It is now self-funding and with the advent of the National Curriculum it has expanded its publications to provide courses throughout Key Stage 3, and for a range of GCSE and A level syllabuses. The project provides INSET for all aspects of National Curriculum, GCSE and A level history, and also publishes *Discoveries*, a journal for history teachers.

Enquiries about the project, INSET and *Discoveries* should be addressed to the Schools History Project, Trinity and All Saints' College, Brownberrie Lane, Horsforth, Leeds LS18 5HD.

Enquiries about the *Discovering the Past* series should be addressed to the publishers, John Murray.

Series consultants
Terry Fiehn
Tim Lomas
Martin and Jenny Tucker

Why choose this depth study?

There are a number of reasons for studying the USA 1919–1941.

- The USA, as the major world superpower, has tremendous influence and power in the world at the end of the twentieth century. It is important to understand its recent history.
- Studying the period is essential to understanding developments in the twentieth century, e.g. the onset of the world-wide Depression in the 1930s.
- Aspects of the period will be familiar to students through television and film so they will find it easy to relate to the materials and period.
- The USA has had a major cultural impact on Britain and other parts of the world, particularly through film and music. Some of the major developments in these areas took place during the period being studied and will help students understand aspects of their own cultural history.
- It provides a context for promoting students' understanding of aspects of historical evidence, particularly the use of film and photography in historical interpretations.
- It includes individuals who have become central characters in the story of the twentieth century, e.g. Henry Ford, Al Capone, Franklin D. Roosevelt.

Aims of *The USA between the Wars 1919–41*

Our aims have been:

- to make this fascinating and relevant area of history accessible to all
- to provide an interesting and motivating course for students and teachers
- to provide thorough exam preparation for all GCSE syllabuses which include this topic
- to provide ample material for in-depth study and for coursework
- to develop students' ability to do the work of a historian: to organise their historical ideas and findings, to ask their own questions, to collect and record information, and to present their results using a range of different techniques.

Structure

The book is divided into four sections.

- Section 1 (Was the USA the land of opportunity?) provides an introduction to American institutions and the make-up of the population. It also considers how the USA emerged from the First World War.
- Section 2 (The USA in the 1920s: Was this a good time for all?) looks at different aspects of America in the 1920s including the economic boom, the extent of poverty, and the widespread intolerance which was a marked feature of the period.
- Section 3 (Crash and Depression) focuses on the events which led up to the Wall Street Crash of 1919 and the onset of the Great Depression of the 1930s; it also looks at the effects of the Depression on Americans.
- Section 4 (Did Roosevelt save America?) examines the effectiveness of Roosevelt and the New Deal in trying to deal with the impact of the Depression on the US economy and thousands of Americans.

Each section is broken down into chapters which roughly correspond to the areas of enquiry suggested by the key questions and focus points of the major exam syllabuses.

The staple of each chapter is **clear explanation** of the core together with **major Tasks and Activities** to help develop students' understanding of the content and their ability to deploy their knowledge. Many of these are supported by this Teachers' Resource Book. Most chapters include material for possible coursework assignments (see below) and in-depth treatment of selected topics to extend students' knowledge and understanding of the period.

Organising your course

We have attempted to cover the requirements of a range of syllabuses and to do so in depth. This means that there is more in this book than you will use in any one GCSE course.

Your approach to teaching this unit and your selection of what to cover will be based on the requirements of your own syllabus. We cannot go into the distinctive requirements of each syllabus here, since they vary in content, focus, case studies and assessment arrangements. This book is particularly closely geared to the content and assessment requirements of the Midland Examining Group's Modern World History syllabus.

This is a book of layers. It contains essential core material which all students should cover; this not only covers content requirements but also each area of the assessment objectives. Other sections look at interesting historical aspects of the history of the period: they could be omitted or used for in-depth coursework. All of the materials can be simplified in the ways suggested below. The core material includes:

- How was the USA governed? (pp. 12–13)
- The 1920s, including the extent of the boom, who did not benefit from the boom, changing attitudes and values (pp. 20–39)

- How widespread was intolerance in the 1920s? (pp. 44–57)
- Prohibition (pp. 58–63)
- What were the causes and consequences of the Wall Street Crash? (pp. 68–73)
- How did the Depression affect urban and rural Americans? (pp. 74–84)
- Why was Roosevelt elected in 1932? (pp. 90–98)
- The New Deal (pp. 100–113)
- Assessment of the New Deal (pp. 116–122).

There is another layer of materials which are not essential but which enhance students' feel for the period, as well as developing particular historical skills. These topics include:

- Coming to America (pp. 4–6)
- Who are the Americans? (pp. 10–11)
- Al Capone (pp. 64–65)
- Novels and documentary photographs of the Depression (pp. 83–87)
- Was America on the brink of revolution? (pp. 91–93)
- Was Roosevelt good for America in the 1930s? (pp. 123–125).

All of the materials, whether in the first or second category above, can be simplified or cut down to save on time, according to the audience and examination pressure.

1. Some sections could be read and discussed in class with little or no written work being done. Examples:

- Coming to America and push/pull factors (pp. 4–9)
- Who are the Americans? (pp. 10–11)
- How could you become President? (pp. 14–15)
- In what ways did the US economy boom in the 1920s? (pp. 22–25)
- Al Capone (pp. 64–65)
- Novels and documentary photographs of the Depression (pp. 83–87).

2. Sections can be truncated. Quite often the first part of an enquiry is text, giving information with supporting sources, then further lines of thought are developed through additional sources. Some of these sources could be cut. Examples:

- For Henry Ford, you could just cover his story, the importance of mass production and the impact of the Model T. (pp. 29–32)
- In 'Why did they execute Sacco and Vanzetti?' (pp. 47–49) and 'What was the Monkey Trial all about?' (pp. 56–57), the main text covers the core syllabus requirements; the sources could be used for extension work.

3. Work can be split up between members of the class in not so essential units to cover them quickly and/or provide a class dynamic. For example:

- In the section on intolerance in the 1920s, different groups of students could cover different topics (Sacco and Vanzetti, Monkey Trial, Ku Klux Klan, the Black Experience) and present their findings to the rest of the class. All students could do the review task on intolerance.

4. Some of the enquiries can be used as extension work for the more able while other students concentrate on core work. For example:

- Was America on the brink of revolution? (pp. 91–93)
- Was Roosevelt good for America in the 1930s? (pp. 123–125)

Using the material in the classroom

The tasks

The book is split into a number of discrete enquiries. Some are short (a single page), while others – particularly those which are tackling the central concerns of the syllabus – are much longer and might provide two or three weeks' work. In these longer enquiries, there are usually a number of tasks *en route* and then a major piece of work at the end (in a blue-ruled box).

The questions and discussions during the rest of the enquiry are an important part of the process of getting ready to tackle these summary tasks. There are, of course, many other questions that could be asked, particularly routine comprehension questions to test understanding. These have been left to the teacher as part of the daily business of teaching. Many of these will be done orally to draw out points of understanding or of interpretation. In this respect, especially in the analysis and interpretation of pictorial sources, teachers may want to ask a whole battery of short questions.

The main purpose of the summary tasks is to show how students have brought together a range of skills and understanding. However, they are also crucial for exam preparation. Many will give invaluable experience not only in recalling and organising knowledge but also in creating a bank of work students can use for revision.

In most questions, the reasons students give for their answers are as important as the answers themselves. In explaining why they have answered in a certain way, they will reveal how deeply they have understood an issue. We have not, however, constantly reiterated in the questions 'explain your answer', as it gets highly repetitive. Students at GCSE level should be well aware that all historical answers require backing up by evidence. However, you might want to remind students of this more often than we have done.

Preparation

Before starting out on an enquiry, always read the questions and activities in the Students' Book and the descriptions and suggestions in this Teachers' Book in the detailed notes on pages 7 to 25. Make sure the students know the ultimate aims of the enquiry or of any piece of work they are undertaking.

A lot of tasks require group work, and many suggest the use of display or presentations. All these have implications for how you organise your classroom.

Sources

Sources are an integral part of the book – some spreads consist of almost nothing but sources. They are designed to be used; many of the questions within an enquiry are designed to ensure that students read, study and understand the source material provided, acquiring source-evaluation skills in the process.

Consistent with our aim of providing useful learning experiences for the students, we have translated, simplified and edited written source material to make it accessible. Make it clear to students that spelling and punctuation have been made contemporary. Modern equivalent words have been substituted where necessary, or definitions provided. Major edits have usually been shown by ellipses. However, the sense and meaning of all sources have been preserved.

The source line – which introduces and describes the source being studied – is an important tool for the student. It contains the details that students will need to know to answer any questions, such as who made or wrote the source and when. Encourage students to see these source lines as an important part of the evidence.

Timelines

This unit may only cover a short period but a chronological overview is still important. Have a large class timeline on the wall on which key characters, events and developments can be displayed. Colour code the different eras. Use it to display students' work.

Differentiation

The questions and activities in the Students' Book are designed to be accessible to all abilities, and the worksheets in this book give further support in the form of writing frames, grids and essay structures. The detailed notes from page 7 onwards also suggest alternative teaching strategies which may help weaker students. However, some more general advice on differentiation may also be helpful.

First-hand classroom experience of teaching from SHP's *Discovering the Past* series has made it clear that students of all abilities can tackle the type of questions and issues in this book, *provided that they are not overwhelmed by being given too many sources, and that the sources they do use are of a suitable level of difficulty.*

One successful approach with mixed ability classes is to have all students attempting the same tasks but to reduce the amount of source material for some of them. This can be done in a number of ways.

- You can divide the class into groups and ask each group to consider just one or two sources. The groups' findings can then be pooled.
- Some groups can use just one source and others can use all the sources. This can be quite successfully done if the groups are carefully selected.
- Instead of splitting the class into groups, you can, with careful class management, give individual students different amounts of source material to use.

As a general principle, as soon as it becomes clear that a student is finding a task difficult, the amount of material he/she is asked to use should be reduced. The important principle remains, however, that all students are being posed the same questions, even if the amount of source material they are using is varied.

Strategies such as these should ensure that all students end up succeeding (at their own level) with each of the tasks in the book.

It is also important that students are not left alone to tackle each enquiry. The book has been written with the expectation that much of the material in the authors' text will be introduced by the teacher. It might be that the teacher reads a spread through beforehand and then uses the information it provides to set the scene for students before they proceed to the sources and questions.

It is also sound practice to read and discuss all sources with students. We are attempting to develop students' skills and understanding, which will not be achieved by simply leaving them to get on with the questions by themselves all the time.

Group work can also help here. Some students will contribute to small group discussion, and risk putting forward ideas and answers in a way which they would not do in front of the whole class. We have all seen how students tend to experiment more in small groups, partly because they are not so worried about getting things wrong.

In this course, students are working with some complex content, ideas, skills and problems for much of the time and we should not be surprised if their early attempts to answer a question fall well below what might be regarded as a good answer. However, any genuine attempts to tackle the questions should be encouraged – the teacher can then begin to suggest how such answers could be built on. If students are worried about 'getting it wrong', they will play safe and their progress will be hindered.

Learning trouble spots

It pays to be aware in advance of areas of the course which weaker students find particularly daunting. For example:

Concepts and terminology
- Students can get confused about the distinction between federal and state governments.
- It is useful if students have a basic idea about why companies issue shares and why share prices rise and fall.
- The concept of the free market in American politics can be problematic, as can the concept of *laissez-faire* policies.

Topics and events
- Causes of the Wall Steet Crash and the Depression – problems with understanding the causes of the Crash and how these lead on to the Depression. See notes on this in the relevant section of this Teachers' Resource Book.
- The New Deal – problems in making the New Deal measures interesting.
- The chronology of the 1920s can cause confusion if students do not realise that the various aspects we are studying – Prohibition, rise of gangsters, religious revivalism, Ku Klux Klan, changing attitudes and behaviour etc. – are taking place at the same time and are interrelated. For example, Prohibition has a continuing impact on American society throughout the 1920s.

Coursework

It is in the very nature of the Discovering the Past series and of the SHP approach that students' work in history should be in the form of key questions to be answered, hypotheses to be tested, and problems, issues or controversies to be investigated. You will therefore find that this book gives an abundant range of possible coursework assignments where this aspect of historical work is to the fore.

It is not our intention to analyse here the particular coursework requirements of each syllabus. Rather, it has been our aim in the writing of the book to provide sufficient depth of content and analysis for coursework assignments to be easily set from this book, without teachers needing to research widely or gather material from many other sources.

The essential features of coursework, for all syllabuses, are that students look in depth at an issue, demonstrate their ability to analyse historical situations and show their ability to be independent learners. In summary, they must engage in the historical process and reach their own conclusions. It is this 'real history' quality of coursework which means that so many teachers, ourselves included, find that students produce their best and most rewarding work. One important feature of setting coursework assignments is to have high expectations. Because of its in-depth coverage and its range of activities, there is ample here for you to set a variety of assignments, whatever the ability of your students. For example:

The topic of Prohibition provides a good opportunity to set a range of coursework assignments focusing on the key concepts of cause and consequence, and change. It is particularly good for looking at how the consequences of one set of events can become the causes of other events. Students could look at:

- why the 18th Amendment was passed
- what its consequences were (what changes it brought about in American society)
- why it was repealed.

Coursework targeted on the use of evidence could look at the topic How the Depression affected Americans? A wide range of evidence is a feature of this section of the book, with a specific focus on the use of photographs and novels in history. There are good opportunities to set work assessing selection and deployment of information.

Other topics for coursework could include:

- how America changed in the 1920s (change and continuity)
- why Roosevelt was elected (causation)
- the role and significance of Henry Ford (the role of the individual).
- assessment of the New Deal (for a longer and more detailed piece of coursework focusing on selection and deployment).

DETAILED NOTES

Section 1: Was the USA the land of opportunity?

CHAPTER 1: WHAT WAS LIFE LIKE IN THE LAND OF THE FREE?

Enquiry: Coming to America

Students' Book pp. 4–6
Worksheets 1, 2

This enquiry is designed to ease students into the course and convey the excitement and anxiety felt by immigrants coming to America at the beginning of the twentieth century. It also aims to put across the idea of the USA as a country open to the poor and oppressed from all parts of the world – one of the fundamental planks of American national ideology. This is important in the context of the course since one of the most significant features of the 1920s was the ending of the open-door policy and the growth of widespread hostility to new immigrants.

Worksheet 1 provides a writing frame to support the written task, although teachers may prefer to use this opening section for discussion only. Alternatively, teachers can write their own comprehension questions on the processing procedure and what can be seen in the pictures.

Worksheet 2 is a map of America for students to use during the course. It includes key locations mentioned in the textbook.

Enquiry: Why did people want to come to the 'land of opportunity'?

Students' Book pp. 7–9

This enquiry is designed to help students understand why people have been attracted to America over several centuries. Teachers might like to brainstorm the factors with students before looking at the textbook: some students will be familiar with push/pull factors from geography. As the main **Activity** is straightforward, it could be set as a homework task, and reviewed briefly before beginning the next section.

The push/pull chart on page 9 may require further explanation. In the final column, students are asked to explain why the source represents a push or pull factor. For example, **Source 5** is a 'pull' factor because it is offering land in Iowa and Nebraska at low prices and on credit. Similarly, the Statue of Liberty in **Source 1** is a 'pull' factor because it symbolises freedom and the chance of a new life for poor and oppressed peoples. The idea of this is to encourage students to give reasoned responses by referring directly to sources in their answers.

Enquiry: Who are the Americans?

Students' Book pp. 10–11

The composition of the American population, especially the notion of the 'melting pot', has an important bearing on developments in the 1920s and 1930s and, of course, is still of great relevance today. Teachers could ask students, working in pairs, to research one of the main ethnic American groups and present their findings to the whole class.

One way to convey the diversity of the US population is to give students a list of famous Americans like the ones below and ask them to say what their country of origin was or what country their families are likely to have originated from. Students could add other names of their own. Another idea is to look at the cast list from an American TV programme or movie.

Great Garbo (Sweden)
Albert Einstein (Germany)
Sitting Bull (Native American)
Stan Laurel (England)
John F. Kennedy (Ireland)
Serge Rachmaninoff (Russia)
Martina Navratilova (Czechoslovakia)
Sylvester Stallone (Italy)
Trini Lopez (Mexico)
Bruce Lee (Hong Kong)
Cher – real name Sarkisian (Armenia)
Alexander Graham Bell (Scotland)
Bela Lugosi (Hungary)
Charlie Chaplin (England)

THE USA BETWEEN THE WARS STUDENTS' BOOK P. 12

Enquiry: How was the USA governed?

Students' Book pp. 12–13
Worksheet 3

This spread provides information about the US system of government; it can be used for reference throughout the course. It is particularly relevant when looking at President Roosevelt's struggle with the Supreme Court over the New Deal. One of the key issues raised here is the question of how far a government should interfere in the lives of its citizens. This is a recurring theme throughout the book and marks the main difference between the Republicans (minimum interference) and the Democrats (intervention on behalf of citizens).

Worksheet 3 provides a boxed layout so that students can make brief notes about the main institutions, powers of president, voting rights etc.

Enquiry: How could you become the President?

Students' Book pp. 14–15
Worksheets 4, 5

This spread aims to provide an overview of the different presidents who were in power during the period being studied.

It highlights the distinction between the Republican and the Democrat periods of power. Some students get a little confused about the Republican Presidents in the 1920s as they are often treated as a single block because their main policies remained largely the same throughout the decade.

Worksheet 4 has more detailed information on Harding and Coolidge. Hoover and Roosevelt are covered in more detail in the textbook.

The short **Task** here is designed to point out that, while it might help to come from humble origins, it was almost obligatory to be a white Protestant male.

Worksheet 5 contains details of Presidents since Roosevelt so that students can judge if this pattern has continued up to the present day. The discussion section starts the debate about government interference in the lives of citizens. Teachers should flag this up directly with students as a major issue in the history of the USA which is still hotly debated today.

CHAPTER 2: HOW DID THE USA EMERGE FROM THE FIRST WORLD WAR?

Enquiry: How did the USA emerge from the First World War?

Students' Book pp. 16–18

This enquiry provides a summary of the state of the USA in 1919. As well as showing the economic advantage the USA gained by the war, it introduces the social and economic problems which became a marked feature of the 1920s. The workers in certain industries never recovered from 1919 and their organisations remained weak during the 1920s and wages relatively low despite the increase in prosperity for others.

This spread also looks at the issue of Isolationism to show how the USA was cutting itself off from European problems and why American voted for 'normalcy' and the Republicans. This is linked to the immigration issue and American fears of being swamped by aliens with radical ideas. This is explored in more depth in Section 2 (see the Red Scare and changes in immigration laws).

8 *The USA between the Wars   Teachers' Resource Book*

Section 2: The USA in the 1920s: Was this a good time for all?

CHAPTER 3: TO WHAT EXTENT DID THE AMERICAN ECONOMY BOOM IN THE 1920s?

Enquiry: The richest country in the world!

Students' Book pp. 20–21

This enquiry looks at the statistics supporting the notion of a boom in the 1920s. It is designed to help students develop their skills in interpreting data. **Source 5** is included to make students aware that the wealth generated by the boom was not being evenly generated. This is taken up in more detail in the enquiry 'Why didn't everybody benefit from the boom?'

Enquiry: In what ways did the American economy boom?

Students' Book pp. 22–25
Worksheets 6, 7

The visual sources in this section are used to put across a vivid impression of the 1920s to help students understand the nature of the boom. It shows how the USA was the first country in the world to become a consumer society. The motor car, clearly a very important part of the boom, has not been given much space here. The impact of the car is covered in the section on Henry Ford and in the section called 'Changing attitudes and values'.

Worksheet 6 provides a table to help students understand how much the boom – in terms of new products, physical changes to the landscape (roads, buildings etc), media products – affected people's daily lives.

Worksheet 7 supports the **Task** on page 25. It gives students an idea of how they might begin drawing their own chart. They can simply add to this one or draw their own. Some teachers might prefer their students to do this as a spider diagram linking up the various aspects of the boom and drawing connections. The point of the exercise is for students to understand how the different areas were interrelated.

Enquiry: Why was there an economic boom in the 1920s?

Students' Book pp. 26–28
Worksheet 8

This is a specific focus question on examination syllabuses, so it has been treated analytically rather than as part of the general information on the boom. The enquiry looks at the network of causal factors which brought about the boom. It aims to show how these factors were related and how growth in one area promoted growth in other areas.

Three teaching strategies to help students understand this topic are described below. Students can work in pairs or small groups. The same nine causal statements about the boom are used in the three different methods; these can be found on **Worksheet 8**.

Card-sort activities like these can be used to help students of all ages and abilities to develop their understanding of and familiarity with historical concepts. The students can physically manipulate the cards to develop an argument in a focused way. You may need to check that students understand the factors/statements on the cards.

Method 1

Arrange the cards in the form of a diamond, with the most important reason at the top and the others in descending order of importance to the least important at the bottom (see diagram 1 overleaf). This allows students to put factors they consider of equal importance on the same level. There is, of course, no absolutely correct order, although we may have clear ideas about the more important and the less important factors. The process makes the students debate the relative merits of the factors because they have to allocate each one a position.

Method 2

Ask the students to draw on an A3-sized piece of paper circles, as shown on diagram 2 overleaf, with the key question 'Why was there a boom?' in the centre. There should be room to place the cause cards in the circles. The circles represent different levels of importance:

THE USA BETWEEN THE WARS STUDENTS' BOOK P. 28

- In the circle nearest the centre, students place the factors which they think were most important in causing the boom – those that really stimulated growth and got things moving, e.g. the motor car
- In the next circle, students put factors which they consider less important but which helped the boom develop, e.g. credit.
- In the outside circle, ask them to put the factors which contributed, but not in a direct way, e.g. natural resources.

The advantage of using cards is that students can move them in and out of different circles as they discuss the factors and make their decisions. For instance, most people would put motor cars at the heart of the boom. But what about confidence: some students could put this in the first circle as one of the essential factors promoting expansion; others might put it in second circle as not so important.

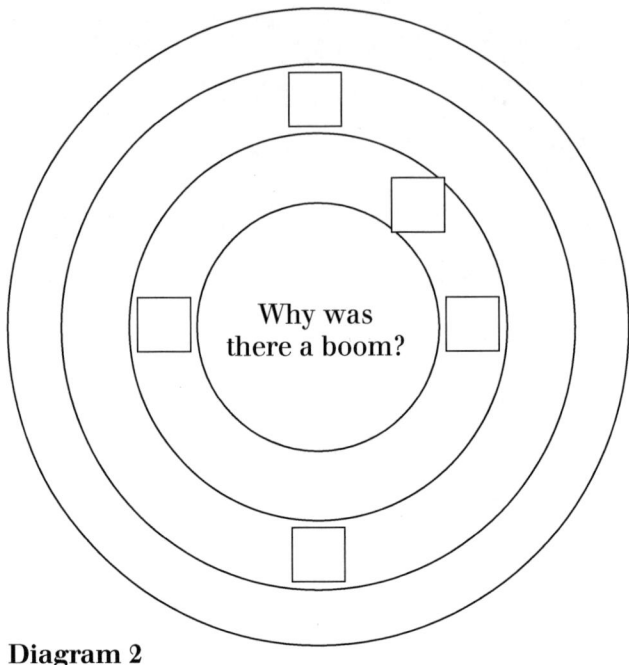
Diagram 2

Method 3

Change the key question to 'Why did the American economy grow so fast in the 1920s?' Ask students to place this statement in the top left-hand corner of the A3-sized piece of paper (see diagram 3). Then ask the students to place the cause cards nearer or further way from the key question, according to how important they think each one was. This gives them more flexibility in weighing up the relative degree of importance. Some positions have been indicated on diagram 3, but these are only to show how cards might be placed and not how they should be placed. It is entirely up to the students. Any cards which they do not consider relevant to the question can be placed off the piece of paper.

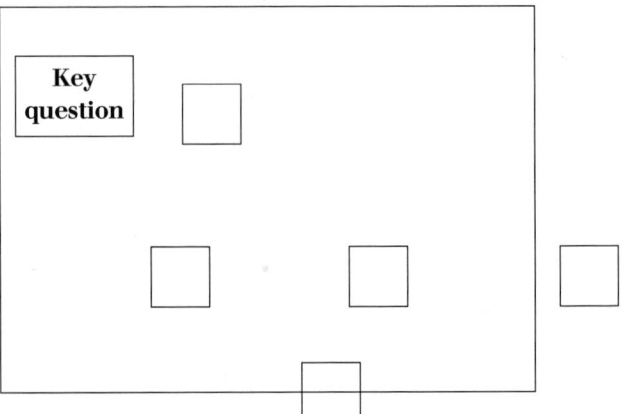
Diagram 3

By changing the key question to focus on the speed of the boom, some factors become more important, particularly credit and advertising. Some factors become less relevant and can be placed off the paper, e.g. natural resources. You could include some blank cards so that students can add their own ideas.

Debriefing the different methods

After the students have completed the exercise, whatever method is adopted, it is important to have a thorough discussion of what conclusions they arrived at and the reasons they give for reaching them. Students do not have to reach agreement. Students can reach different conclusions as long as they are able to justify their conclusions. The placing of the cards allows them to play around with different ideas, change their minds and reformulate before reaching a final conclusion.

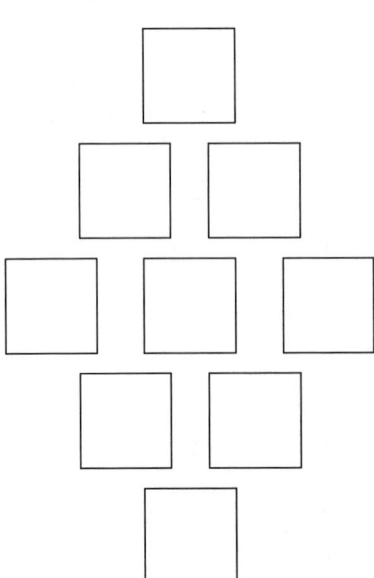
Diagram 1

Teachers may like to use the approach in Method 3 for the key question 'Why was there a boom?' and then ask students how they would change the positions of the cards if asked the question 'Why did the American economy grow so fast in the 1920s?' Changing the questions throws a completely different light on the arrangement of factors and makes the discussion more interesting.

A writing frame is provided on **Worksheet 9** to help students write the essay on page 28 of the textbook. Students can move straight to this after doing the card exercise(s) described above. The task on page 28 also provides an intermediate stage, helping students to write the essay. It can be ignored if teachers have used the card exercises.

The polices of the Republican Presidents

This short section on page 28 of the textbook provides an overview of the policies of the Republicans in the 1920s. More detailed information on the policies can be found on page 27. Two worksheets (see below) provide more depth on the Presidents themselves and their policies.

Worksheet 4 contains profiles of Presidents Harding and Coolidge. These cover their personalities, policies and other points of interest, e.g. the scandals associated with the Harding administration.

Worksheet 10 has a quiz-style decision-making activity 'Would you have made a good Republican president?' This asks students to make judgements about key issues in the 1920s to see if they would have made the same ones as the Republicans. A second sheet (**10**) gives scores and detailed answers about what the Republican Presidents did. This is a good activity for teasing out what Republican policies meant in practice, particularly their emphasis on the free market and non-interference in business. Teachers might like to return to this when they look at the causes of the Depression: Republican refusal to help the farmers and their policy of weakening trade unions helped to create the uneven distribution of wealth in the 1920s which was a major cause of the Depression.

Enquiry: How did Henry Ford make the Ford Motor Car Company the most successful in the world in the 1920s?

Students' Book p. 29

The story strip tells how Henry Ford created the world's biggest motor manufacturing company in the 1920s.

Enquiry: Why is Henry Ford so significant in American history?

Students' book pp. 30–32
Worksheets 11, 12, 13

Henry Ford is one of the most famous names of this century and symbolises the American businessman of the twentieth century. His drive and determination, pioneering spirit and the self-confidence which enabled him to risk everything in bold moves mark him out as an icon of the period. Added to this is his unique mechanical skills, business acumen and capacity for hard work. He also symbolises the harshness of the period – his production line with its heavy toll on workers and his treatment of union sympathisers.

Ford was a significant public figure; his views and opinions carried weight with the public. If he had been more accommodating, he might well have run for an important political post, even the presidency. His anti-Semitism is significant because it encouraged groups like the Ku Klux Klan. In a different sense, his museum of Americana at Greenfields is significant because it has influenced generations of Americans, presenting a very specific perspective on American history.

How much of this you may want to cover depends on the time available. You could simply focus on the impact of the Model T and the importance of mass production techniques.

THE USA BETWEEN THE WARS STUDENTS' BOOK P. 33

Alternatively, the materials could be used for coursework focusing on the role of an individual in history. Some extra sources can be found on **Worksheet 11**. These concentrate on the darker side of his production processes and his relationship with management and workers.

The key question, **Question 8**, at the bottom of page 31 asks students to consider the factors that made Henry Ford a successful businessman. Before they do this, they should be referred back to the story strip on page 29. This brings out his determination to succeed, mechanical abilities, the way he was able to design the right car for the market and his administrative skills in setting up a concern to make cars in large numbers.

Worksheet 12 provides supporting material to help students write the essay on Ford. They have to decide which factors contributed most to his significance in American history.

Method

Ask students to work in pairs or groups. Give them a piece of A3-sized paper and tell them to put the key question 'Why is Henry Ford so significant in American history?' in the top left-hand corner. Then ask them to arrange the significance cards on the paper in positions which they think reflect his significance, with the most important being nearer to the key question (see diagram on page 10 of this Teacher's Resource Book). Any of the cards which are judged not to be significant can be left off the paper, ones marginally significant can be placed half-on and half-off.

This will raise some interesting issues. For instance, most people will see his development of the Model T as one of the most significant factors. But what about his anti–Semitism? This might be seen to be relatively unimportant when compared with his development of the car and his impact on industrial production. But if you were investigating intolerance in the USA in this period, then it would be very significant. The aim here is to encourage students to discuss the relative merits of different factors and develop a clearer understanding of them.

The inclusion of cards which are not significant or of very minor significance helps to increase students' powers of discrimination. It is important for students to realise that some points are not relevant to a particular question posed. A full discussion of the students' conclusions should be encouraged, leading to the final written Task on page 32. A writing frame has been provided on **Worksheet 13** to help students do this.

Enquiry: Why didn't everybody benefit from the boom?

Students' Book pp. 33–35
Worksheet 14

This enquiry looks at the main groups which were disadvantaged in the 1920s. Most space is given over to the farming community because they formed such a large share of the population. Also, low farm incomes affected a much wider group of people who depended on the farmers for their livelihood. The photograph of the combine harvester in **Source 4** helps explain overproduction and why many farm workers and sharecroppers were no longer required to work the land.

The questions and **Task** are designed to highlight the problems in various industries. Mechanisation and overproduction contributed to low wages, putting the different groups below the poverty line. The figure given in the textbook is 42 per cent, but some books put this as high as 60 per cent.

You might also like to point out that Republican governments in the 1920s did not help. Their 'non-interference' policies were disastrous for the farmers. There were several attempts in Congress to guarantee farm prices or raise them (e.g. by buying up surplus produce), but the Republican government refused to support any of these.

The Republicans also helped to drive down wages by weakening the bargaining position of trade unions. They considered that trade unions placed restrictions on businesses and made them uncompetitive. They would not support laws limiting child labour and introducing minimum wages for women. They sanctioned the use of force to suppress strikes. **Worksheet 10** (mentioned above) could be brought in at this point.

Teachers may prefer their students to do a more straightforward task than writing a report. This could be used as an opportunity to teach note-taking to students; they could be encouraged to make notes on the different groups and the reasons why they were poor. **Worksheet 14** will help them do this. This information will be useful when they consider the causes of the Crash and the Depression.

THE USA BETWEEN THE WARS STUDENTS' BOOK P. 45

CHAPTER 4: HOW WAS SOCIETY CHANGING IN THE 1920s?

Enquiry: Changing attitudes and values

Students' Book pp. 36–39

This section looks at the changes in people's attitudes and values, especially issues of morality, in the 1920s. It was a time of great excitement when people indulged in all sorts of unusual activities, such as flagpole-sitting sessions, marathon dances, mah-jong competitions.

The section on Prohibition comes at the end of the material on the 1920s because it is part of the chapter on intolerance. However, an understanding of the impact of Prohibition on American society in the 1920s is important to understanding the changing behaviour, attitudes and values of the period. The glamour of illegal drinking and secret parties gave the decade its extra edge of excitement. Teachers should, therefore, briefly introduce Prohibition before students do this section, perhaps using one of the videos that are available on the USA in the 1920s.

The painting *Entertainment* has been selected as an image for interrogation to look at how paintings can be used by historians. It also encapsulates some of the key aspects of the 1920s in a hard, gritty way. Some questions are suggested in the textbook, but teachers might like to subject it to a barrage of questions on specific characters and parts of the painting to pull out what they reveal.

Some of the main changes in behaviour and attitudes in the 1920s were to do with women and perceptions of their role in society. This is covered in the next enquiry.

Enquiry: How was life different for women in the 1920s?

Students' Book pp. 40–43

The first spread describes some of the main changes for women and sets up the flapper as the extreme model of changing attitudes. It invites students to draw conclusions about how life changed for women in the 1920s. The second spread looks at the extent of the changes for women in general across the USA. It brings in evidence which indicates that these changes were limited for many women; it seems they were carrying out their roles in much the same way as before the war.

The Middletown case study is an optional one for those who want to investigate this area further. The survey reveals a mixed picture. It suggests that women were largely carrying out the same roles, based in the home, as before but that many were also taking on jobs outside, confirming other information that women's position in the workplace was changing. Interestingly, the gap between the attitudes of mothers and their daughters comes out quite clearly, as young women were affected by influences outside the home, such as the cinema.

CHAPTER 5: HOW WIDESPEAD WAS INTOLERANCE IN THE 1920s?

Enquiry: The Red Scare

Students' Book pp. 44–45
Worksheet 15

The Red Scare in the early 1920s is comparable with the anti-Communism of the McCarthy era after the Second World War. The Scare was a period of near-hysteria whipped up by the press at a time of social tension. This had been brought about by problems of dislocation caused by the war and other social changes. The migration of black people to northern cities and the very high rates of immigration before the war had created ghettos and social problems in the cities. Workers, whose rates of pay had been kept very low during the war, felt it was time to make the case of organised labour. This led to a wave of strikes including a general strike in Seattle. A series of bombings heightened these tensions.

With little evidence of revolutionary activities to justify it, the resultant crackdown by the authorities was an over-the-top reaction. However, the Scare had far-reaching implications for the rest of the decade. It led to growing support for organisations like the American Legion and the Ku Klux Klan, dedicated to protecting 'true' American values and crushing foreigners and others – Jews, Catholics, Communists etc – who seemed to be undermining them. The idea of one-hundred-per-cent Americanism had widespread support in the press and among the general public.

Worksheet 15 contains two cartoons from the period which can be used to help students understand these attitudes.

Teachers might like to draw connections with present-day events in America, for instance, the rise of far-right militia groups. The views these groups are espousing are those of one-hundred-per-cent Americanism. They want a return to the 'true' pioneering white values of the nineteenth century.

THE USA BETWEEN THE WARS STUDENTS' BOOK P. 46

The questions try to bring out the attitudes of the time, particularly the over-reaction of the media. Questions 5 and 6 are quite difficult.

Question 5 deals with the interesting idea that the right-wing groups carried out the bombings to discredit left-wing groups and increase public antagonism towards them.

Question 6, then looks at an anarchist pamphlet (**Source 5**) found near the scene of one of the bombings. Sophisticated students might point out that this pamphlet may have been written and planted by right-wing groups. This should promote some interesting discussion.

Enquiry: How and why did immigration policy change in the 1920s?

Students' Book p. 46

This carries on the theme of the previous enquiry. The government response to the public feeling that America was being swamped by foreigners was to cut down the number of people allowed entry. This should not be seen entirely in terms of prejudice against newcomers. Immigration before the war was the highest it had ever been and there was social instability in the big northern cities. Many people who did not share the prejudiced views of those in the **Sources** on page 46 felt that it was necessary to control immigration to allow a chance for the new wave of immigrants to be assimilated.

Enquiry: Why were Sacco and Vanzetti executed?

Students' Book pp. 47–49
Worksheet 16

The Sacco and Vanzetti case is a famous example of the injustice which accompanied the intolerance of the 1920s. The enquiry title has been chosen to highlight the notion that Sacco and Vanzetti were probably executed because of who they were rather than because they were guilty. It seems likely that they were convicted because they were Italian anarchists. It is important that students understand the context in which the trial took place, i.e an atmosphere of hysteria about foreign radicals.

The initial page tells the story to set the context for the source investigation. The sources then allow students to investigate the trial in more detail and draw some conclusions for themselves. The trial details are designed to show the inconclusive nature of the evidence and also how a large number of witnesses supporting Sacco and Vanzetti were ignored. This having been said, students might suggest that these witnesses were not reliable because they were Italians and on the side of Sacco and Vanzetti.

Question 6 has been designed to help students consider possible reasons why Sacco and Vanzetti were found guilty and executed. This should not be seen as a simple choice: students should be encouraged to use a combination of reasons. The important aspect of the answer is their justification for these reasons.

The sources do clearly point in one direction and this is the result of this author's selection which reflects the conclusions of most historians. We are not in a position to judge whether Sacco and Vanzetti were guilty or not but we can have an opinion on the fairness of their trial. In this respect the historical evidence points to the prejudice of the judge, the bias in the jury and the dubious nature of the evidence at the trial.

One approach, if teachers wish to set a longer writen task on this topic, is to ask students to present a 'Rough Justice' style TV programme on the trial. This could simply be a piece of writing representing the script for the programme, or groups of students could stage the programme for the rest of the class. Support for this is provided on **Worksheet 16**.

Enquiry: The rise and fall of the Ku Klux Klan

Students' Book pp. 50–52
Worksheet 17

The Klan was largely composed of Americans who were concerned that their WASP values were being eroded by foreigners and other ethnic and religious groups. This enquiry looks at why the Klan got so much support in the 1920s. The first part of the **Source Investigation** on page 51 focuses on some of their main ideas and beliefs. These include the ideas of white Protestant supremacy linked with 'true' American values. This is why the Klan identifies with the American flag and patriotism. The Klan believed these Protestant Christian values were under attack from Catholics, Jews and Socialists etc. The work students have done on the Red Scare should help them understand this.

THE USA BETWEEN THE WARS STUDENTS' BOOK P. 55

Worksheet 17 contains more information on the beliefs and organisation of the Klan which students should find interesting.

You may wish to draw parallels with increasing nationalism and racism in the world today. In a more humorous vein, it is tempting to suggest that the fear of aliens (eastern and southern European immigrants) prevalent in the 1920s has been replaced in the USA today by fear of aliens of the outer space variety. Is this a line of historical continuity?

Question 1 is designed to get students to consider some of the more obvious aspects of the Klan – secret meetings, frightening and intimidating uniforms and so on. While amusing at first glance, the photograph showing the small child is sinister, suggesting, as it does, that the Klan represented a value system into which children were indoctrinated. Teachers will probably need to ask a series of more specific questions to draw out some of these points in a question and answer session.

The second part of the **Source Investigation** on page 52 focuses on KKK methods. The Klan is associated with the persecution of black people, but it had a wider range of targets. These involved beating up strikers, whipping women and men who were thought to have engaged in immoral behaviour, attacking Jews and so on. Teachers might like to ask students why they think so few Klan members were caught and punished for their crimes? (Many of the Klan were members of police forces or held powerful political positions.)

Enquiry: The black experience in the 1920s

Students' Book pp. 53–55
Worksheets 18, 19

This enquiry has a number of purposes: to give information about the position of black people in America, to draw attention to the Black Renaissance in Harlem and make students aware of the political movements that fed into the civil rights and Black Power movements of the 1960s and 1970s.

It is very easy in the short generalised histories of the USA at GCSE level to see black people only in powerless positions, the subject of white intimidation and violence. The notorious Rosewood story, which can be found on **Worksheet 18**, shows the effects of white violence and black resistance to it. But there were very strong and vibrant movements in black society which reveal a totally different picture. The Black Renaissance in Harlem is one of these. There was a flowering of talent in many directions – art, music literature – which had a great impact on American society. Jazz and the blues have been a major influence on American music since the 1920s. Teachers might like to get their students to carry out further research on key figures in the Black Renaissance. A profile of James Weldon Johnson can be found on **Worksheet 19**.

Marcus Garvey and W.E.B DuBois represent different strands of Black protest: Garvey (profile on **Worksheet 18**) represents the separatist approach evident in the later Black Power movement, DuBois the more integrationist approach seen in the later civil rights movement. Both, however, stressed links with Africa and pride in Black culture.

The **Task** at the end of this section gives students a choice of written work. They can either do a more straightforward exercise looking at change and continuity for black Americans in the 1920s or a more complex activity where they examine these changes through different stances in the black community. The second activity is substantially more demanding; teachers may like to use this to differentiate between students of different abilities.

Also included in this section is a short account of the situation for Native American Indians which presents a gloomy picture of ill-treatment and lack of understanding.

The **Activity** at the end encourages students to put together some ideas on the intolerance in American society in the 1920s. Teachers may prefer to leave this until after the material on religious intolerance or after the initial section on Prohibition, as this can be seen as an aspect of the intolerance which characterises the 1920s. It is suggested that this is done in groups as it involves students looking back over a substantial number of pages in the textbook and would benefit from group discussion about choice of material and supporting evidence for the radio programme.

THE USA BETWEEN THE WARS STUDENTS' BOOK P. 56

Enquiry: What was the Monkey Trial all about?

Students' Book pp. 56–57
Worksheet 20

Before tackling the Monkey Trial, teachers might like students to consider in more detail the religious revivalism taking place in the 1920s. **Worksheet 20** has information and tasks on this.

The title of the enquiry is meant to signify that the trial was not just about teaching the theory of evolution; it was about different groups trying to publicise their views – Christian fundamentalists on the one hand and a civil liberties organisation on the other. Both saw the trial as a forum to put their views to a much wider audience. In the end, although the defendant Scopes was found guilty, it was the civil liberties group which could claim victory because fundamentalist ideas had been ridiculed.

Question 1 raises the issue of parental control over what is taught in schools (schools in America in the 1920s were funded locally and at state level). If teachers do not wish to set the letter as a task, then comprehension questions can be set on the sources and text pulling out the reasons why people wanted a law banning the teaching of the theory of evolution. Teachers might like to take the discussion further and consider how far parents should control what is taught in British Schools today.

Enquiry: Prohibition – a noble experiment or a national disaster?

Students' Book pp. 58–59
Worksheet 21

This section has been included in the chapter on intolerance because the anti-drinking lobby represents the broad moral/religious front which was trying to keep America a pure, simple, hard-working and clean-living country. The questions ask students to consider the reasons put forward in support of Prohibition and to work out why the 18th Amendment was passed.

Worksheet 21 is a role-play that looks at who might have supported Prohibition in 1918 and also how these people may/may not have changed their opinions by 1933. There are eight characters who can be distributed among the class. Teachers can add more characters if they wish or students could invent some of their own.

The question 'Do you support Prohibition?' can be put in 1918 after students have done the work on this section. The same question can be repeated after students have completed the work on the next enquiry, supposing it were 1933. The expected outcome is that:

- in 1933 some groups will change their opinion and vote against Prohibition
- other groups will vote the same way as they did in 1918.

Enquiry: Why didn't Prohibition work?

Students' Book pp. 60–63
Worksheet 22

This enquiry has a strong narrative section at the beginning to try to capture the spirit of the period. Students are then led into sources which focus on the reasons why Prohibition failed. These highlight the lack of public support for Prohibition and the problems of stopping the illegal liquor trade, especially the problem of corruption.

There are many interesting aspects to the story of Prohibition, particularly the involvement of big business with the suppliers of illegal liquor. There are also any number of amusing, tragic or strange stories which have contributed to the legend of the Prohibiton era. One of the strangest is the story of Two-gun Hart. Operating in old-fashioned cowboy style in Nebraska, Hart was amazingly successful in locating stills and stopping the illegal liquor trade, his career being brought to an end by corrupt officials in high places. But what is really odd is that he was the son of an Italian immigrant, who had dreamt of the Wild West as a child, and that he was the brother of Al Capone.

At the end of the enquiry, the focus shifts to why Prohibition was ended. This cannot be clearly disentangled from why it failed, but there is a greater emphasis on the consequences of Prohibition for American society, particularly the growth of organised crime and the corruption of local, state and federal government officials. It was a high price to pay for the so-called 'noble experiment' and teachers might like to discuss this with students, referring to the issue of drug-taking in society today. Another interesting aspect to look at is the role of women in getting Prohibition passed and then getting it repealed. **Worksheet 22** provides support for students writing the essay.

Enquiry: The Story of Al Capone

Students' Book pp. 64–65
Worksheet 23

Al Capone has been chosen as the main focus for the gangster era because he is the very epitome of the American gangster. His early career shows how gangsters gained a position of power in the first place; his 'star' billing shows the ambivalence of the public's response to gangsters; his use of intimidation, violence and corruption shows how gangsterism debased American society. This enquiry is constructed to bring out these points so that students can put gangsters in a clear historical context rather than just see them as an episode in American history.

Worksheet 23 contains accounts of the careers of three other gangsters. The tasks are designed to show the similarities in their backgrounds and their routes to power so that they can be seen as a historical rather than individual phenomenon. The film the *Roaring Twenties*, with James Cagney, is useful for analysing how bootlegging led to gangsterism and why certain types of people became involved in it.

Review: Were the 1920s a good time for the USA?

Students' Book p. 66

The **Review Task** provides a good opportunity to look back at the material on the 1920s and give overall shape to the period. The task aims to help students appreciate that the experience of the 1920s varied considerably according to the colour, class and location of particular groups of people.

Teachers could take an different angle on this and return to the theme of chapter one, 'What was it like in the land of opportunity?' Teachers could ask students to discuss how far America really was the land of the free and how far it measured up to immigrants' expectations of it. This ties in with the idea of the review task because the 1920s were a decade of freedom and opportunity for some, but not for others. This also, perhaps more directly, focuses on the wave of intolerance which restricted the freedom of some groups socially, politically and economically.

Section 3: Crash and Depression

CHAPTER 6: WHAT WERE THE CAUSES AND CONSEQUENCES OF THE WALL STREET CRASH?

Enquiry: What was the Wall Street Crash?

Students' Book pp. 68–69

This enquiry gives students essential information about the Crash of October 1929. Students should know what happened and have a working knowledge of the operation of share prices and how speculation was based on borrowing ('on the margin'). The separate panel on shares provides a brief summary, and teachers may prefer to cover this in more detail with a more practical demonstration of how share prices go up and down. This can be done by giving (selling) some shares to students and then introducing different market conditions, asking them if they want to buy and sell.

The questions on page 69 are intended to draw out some key points about how it happened. The newspaper front page presents a more dynamic framework to enable students to cover what happened and identify some of the consequences for individuals. This could be done in groups, with different students contributing to the different sections of the front page.

Enquiry: What were the causes of the Wall Street Crash?

Students' Book pp. 70–71
Worksheet 24

This is possibly the most difficult part of the course for many students and will require a great deal of supporting explanation from teachers. The causes of the Crash are identified as overcapacity and speculation. These have been broken down into more manageable chunks – overproduction, distribution of income, lack of markets and so on. The idea of using long-term/short-term causes is to help students realise that some of the causes had been building up for some time, e.g. unfair income distribution in the USA and shrinking markets overseas.

At this level, all we can expect in the written explanation is a clear statement of how each factor contributed. Any students who can take this further and show an understanding of the interrelationship of the factors and be able to make qualified statements about them are working at a high level. What is important is that they realise that it is not just speculation that caused the Crash – some students are inclined to take this as the sole explanation. **Worksheet 24** supports the written task.

Enquiry: Why did the Wall Street Crash lead to the Great Depression?

Students' Book pp. 70–73

The Crash triggered the Depression. It brought an immediate collapse in marginal enterprises in business, farming and banking (many of which were already on the point of collapse before the Crash) and launched America into the Depression at breakneck speed. However, some historians have pointed out that the Depression was well under way by the time of the Crash, the economy having shown a marked downturn in the summer of 1929.

The underlying causes of the Depression were the same as those which brought about the Crash. This spread shows how problems in various sectors of the US economy contributed to the onset of the Depression. The Task on page 73 helps students to understand that the Crash made things worse by triggering bank failures and cutbacks in production leading to unemployment which in turn led to falling demand, factory closures etc. – a vicious downward spiral. It does not really matter in which order the phrases go as long as they make sense and show this spiral process.

CHAPTER 7: THE EFFECTS OF THE DEPRESSION

Enquiry: How did the Depression affect people in the cities?

Students' Book pp. 74–77
Worksheet 25

This enquiry is largely an information-gathering exercise for students to use sources to gain understanding of the impact of the Depression on masses of Americans. The main **Activity** at the end is designed to help students record some of the information in brief note form. This could be turned into an extended written response. **Worksheet 25** contains more information about the position of black people in the Depression.

THE USA BETWEEN THE WARS STUDENTS' BOOK P. 87

Enquiry: Did the Depression affect all urban Americans?

Students' Book p. 78

This single-page enquiry raises the question about whether all people were affected by the Depression. Otherwise students may feel that everybody was going through similar experiences. The majority of Americans remained in jobs, although many took cuts in pay etc. The rich, on the whole, remained rich. Their wealth was usually held in a variety of assets, not just stocks and shares. There were, of course, examples of rich people losing everything in the Crash.

The point is made in the later sources that psychologically, especially in small towns, most people were affected because they knew people who had lost jobs and were suffering, and this caused anxiety and insecurity. Also the Depression did cut across most classes of people, so previously well-off Americans could and did find themselves destitute.

Enquiry: How did the Depression affect people in the countryside

Students' Book 79–80

The situation of farmers in the Depression is similar to that described in the 1920s – overproduction, low prices, low incomes etc. – so this is not covered again. The focus in the enquiry is, therefore, on the sources. **Source 1** is particularly important because it describes the dilemma in American society – people starving while food is being thrown away because prices are too low. It is worth taking students through this source carefully. **Source 3** opens up the discussion of reliablity of evidence because the writer has a political agenda. However, it also shows students that a source which has a clear bias can provide useful information when it is supported by other evidence.

Enquiry: The Dust Bowl

Students' Book p. 81

The section on the Dust Bowl provides the factual background for understanding why there was such a massive migration from parts of the Midwest in the 1930s. It looks at how farmers in a large part of the Midwest farming belt were affected by a part natural/part man-made disaster.

Enquiry: Migrants

Students' Book pp. 82–84

This enquiry focuses on the use of the historical novel in history. *The Grapes of Wrath* by John Steinbeck is used as a historical source and provides, for many Americans, the main account on which their interpretation of this period of American history is based. So, this is a good opportunity to consider the novel as evidence.

The novel is a combination of descriptive passages and the fictional story of the Joads. Steinbeck spent several months on research and lived with migrants for some of this time. Although there are obvious exaggerations for dramatic effect, much of the detail, it would seem, remains accurate and well observed. In fact, there are suggestions that Steinbeck underplayed some of the things described in the novel. The book does have its critics who claim it distorts the facts and is hopelesly romantic. Oklahomans themselves have criticised the portrayal of their fellows as backward, simple-minded and ill-educated. Others maintain the book is campaigning propaganda by Steinbeck, overstating his case to try to shock the authorities into action to help the migrants.

The questions here are designed to try to pull out students' ideas in a structured way so that they can draw some considered conclusions rather than give a standardised answer. They should be able to say that despite reservations, some novels are more useful than others because of the research carried out by the author and his or her depth of knowledge. In the end, the key test is confirmation from a range of other sources and students should be guided in this direction if they have not reached it themselves.

As an additional resource, extracts from the film *The Grapes of Wrath* can be used; it should be noted that some parts are different from the book.

Enquiry: Documentary photographs of the Depression

Students' Book pp. 85–87

Like the previous enquiry, this one focuses on a specific aspect of historical evidence – photographs. These are famous photographs, ones that for many years have seemed to capture the very essence of the Depression in rural America. They were taken by photographers such as Walker Evans, Dorothea Lange and Margaret Bourke-White. They are icons of the

The USA between the Wars Teachers' Resource Book

period and have formed the main visual base for many people's interpretation of the impact of the Depression on the migrants and farm workers. Historically, therefore, they are very important.

Many of them were commissioned by the Farm Securities Administration as a visual record of the period. This would seem to make them visual sources of the highest order for the historian, almost unchallengeable. However, William Stott, who knew and talked to many of the photographers, shows in his excellent book, *Documentary Expression and Thirties America*, that the photogaphers had a clear agenda. They carefully posed the photographs to convey a particular 'look' to their audiences, of people down on their luck but who faced hardship with dignity and would weather the storm. Sometimes they waited hours to capture this look. More than this, there is a question of the selection of photographs that were shown to the public audience. They did not select photographs of people doing normal things – children playing, people dancing or enjoying themselves, getting dressed up to go to church on Sunday etc.

The questions in this enquiry are designed to draw out some of the points mentioned above, although they might need more support and discussion from teachers. The point is also made in the last question that, despite these reservations, some of these photographs convey images of the Midwest and the people that it would be very difficult to convey in words.

The final **Activity** asks students to select a very limited number of photographs which capture the essence of the Depression. This should help them to understand that selection is a crucial part of the history presented by historians to their audiences. This might also be a good opportunity to look back at the photographs in this whole section on the Depression to consider their usefulness as evidence.

Enquiry: Why were the 1930s a golden age for Hollywood?

Students' Book pp. 88–89

The enquiry looks at the success of the cinema in the 1930s. It shows how the cinema offered people comfort and a touch of luxury in the hard world of the Depression. Films were now 'talkies' and some, by the end of the 1930s, were in colour. The audience could feel that they were in touch with the stars themselves through magazines. It is perhaps not surprising that cinema attendance soared.

The last question considers the usefulness of films as evidence. Although the films of the 1930s have, in the main, limited usefulness as documentation of the events of the period, they do provide insights into aspects of social life like clothes and customs and attitudes to people. The film, *The Grapes of Wrath*, on the other hand, contains scenes which tell us much about the migrant experience. However, it is interesting that the film's producers changed the ending to make it more upbeat than that of the book.

CHAPTER 8: WHY WAS FRANKLIN D. ROOSEVELT ELECTED PRESIDENT IN 1932?

Enquiry: What action did Hoover's government take to deal with the Depression?

Students' Book p. 90

This enquiry provides essential information about the actions of the Republican government (required for most exam syllabuses) as a backdrop to an examination of anti-government feeling.

Enquiry: Protest – was America on the brink of revolution?

Students' Book pp. 91–93

There were violent confrontations between the authorities and protesters, particularly the Bonus Marchers, and there was a lot of talk about revolution from various groups. People were disillusioned and angry, and, in similar circumstances, the Nazis rose to power in Germany. This puts the subsequent achievements of Roosevelt in a clearer light: we can see why some commentators have said that he saved democracy in America.

The sources here provide scope for evaluation, as most of the commentators have personal or political agendas. MacArthur in **Source 3** seeks to justify his own actions saying that the Bonus March was a serious threat to the government. The authors of **Sources 5, 6** and **7** may be playing up the idea of revolution to make the government do something about the plight of the farmers. The Communist writer in **Source 8** has a clear interest in suggesting revolution as the only route for workers.

Source 9 puts the issue into context. It was unlikely that a revolution would have taken place; most people just wanted jobs and relief.

However, there might have been serious challenges to authority in many places. America in the 1930s remained a violent society, especially in respect of labour union activity. It is easy to underestimate this because Roosevelt was successful in holding things together.

Enquiry: The 1932 election

Students' Book pp. 94–96

As students work through this and the following enquiry, it is very helpful if they use a chart like that suggested in **Question 3** on page 95. This will give direction and purpose to their reading. They can begin to work out what factors were working in Roosevelt's favour, including negative perceptions of Hoover. The **Task** on page 96 helps students to establish what the candidates' positions and policies were. An optional activity – to design a campaign poster for Roosevelt – is included on page 97.

Enquiry: Why did Roosevelt win the election?

Students' Book pp. 97–98
Worksheet 26

By the time students come to the end of this section, they should have collected a lot of evidence for their essay. **Worksheet 26** provides an activity to help students structure their essays.

This activity helps students to distinguish main points from supporting evidence or explanation. Students have to select the main points first of all and then find the supporting points (evidence or explanation) that fit these main points.

Teachers will have to decide how much of this they need to use, depending on the ability and essay-writing skills of their students. Some might just want to use the main points and get students to brainstorm or develop for themselves the supporting points. Others might want them to do the full activity and then leave students to deploy the information themselves. Some students will need help in structuring the essay and deploying the information.

Running the activity

- Arrange students in pairs or small groups.
- Give each pair or group a set of cards which have been cut up and jumbled up. Tell them to spread out the cards on the table (desk) in front of them.
- Ask students to decide what the main points are (see below). Help any groups which are having difficulty.
- Tell students to put these points across the table to form a series of columns. Then ask them to sort the other cards into the columns by deciding which of the main points they support or explain, i.e. the main point should be at the top of the column and the supporting points underneath. The columns do not have to contain the same number of points.
- Students can be asked to contribute other points of their own, creating a new column or just adding extra supporting points. They can then use these columns to structure their essays.

The main points are:

- Roosevelt and the Democrats had positive policies for dealing with the Depression
- Roosevelt's personality and the way he conducted his campaign persuaded people to vote for him
- Hoover was very unpopular
- Republican policies had not been acceptable to the American people.

Section 4: Did Roosevelt save America?

CHAPTER 9: THE NEW DEAL

Enquiry: The Hundred Days

Students' Book pp. 100–101

This spread introduces the main aims of the New Deal and describes how Roosevelt began his presidency. It then looks at Roosevelt's efforts to gain the trust of Americans and stabilise the banking system. In the last weeks of Hoover's administration, the banking system was in serious trouble; some big banks were on the point of collapse. Roosevelt's measures to stabilise the banks were welcomed by business as a necessary survival measure. The importance of restoring confidence in the banks, thereby preventing further economic collapse, is often overlooked in assessments of the New Deal.

Enquiry: The alphabet agencies

Students' Book pp. 102–104

This enquiry provides essential information about the New Deal agencies. To access this information in an active way, it is suggested that students start with the the chart on page 104. **Worksheet 27** has a full-page chart for students to fill in as they work through the measures.

Another approach would be to break the agencies up into categories and ask students to write brief notes for each, explaining what the agencies did and how they were designed to help people. For example:

- Which agencies gave relief to people?
- Which agencies helped farmers?
- Which agencies helped the unemployed?
- Which agencies helped businesses and workers?

Enquiry: How was the Second New Deal different from the First?

Students' Book pp. 105–107
Worksheet 27

Students should add details about the Second New Deal to the chart they start for the alphabet agencies. They could do the **Review Activity** on pages 106 and 107 as they are doing the chart. This will give more interest and purpose to students reading the details of the acts and agencies.

The answers to the **Review Activity** on pages 106–107 are as follows:

Source 1 – CWA
Source 2 – CCC
Source 3 – FERA
Source 4 – AAA
Source 5 – PWA
Source 6 – WPA
Source 7 – NRA

Enquiry: Why did Roosevelt win the biggest ever landslide victory in the presidential election of 1936?

Students' Book pp. 108–109

To a large extent, this enquiry is concerned with an assessment of Roosevelt's qualities as a leader and his relationship with the American people. His leadership style appealed to ordinary people; they felt he was really trying to help them in a way other governments in the past had not. If teachers wish to set a different activity, they could ask students to write an election speech for Roosevelt. This could stress the different groups of people the New Deal agencies had helped and what had been achieved since 1933.

Enquiry: Who did not support the New Deal?

Students' Book pp. 110–113
Worksheets 28, 29

This enquiry looks at the various groups who opposed the New Deal. The questions on the first spread are targeted at the interpretation of political cartoons and their use as evidence. The cartoon showing Roosevelt steering the ship may need some explanation as students have, at this point, not done any work on the conflict between Roosevelt and the Supreme Court (see page 114). Teachers should point out that the compass represents the Supreme Court and the sailor represents Congress and explain why some people saw Roosevelt as acting in a dictatorial fashion.

The **Task** gives students a chance to express the main criticisms from the three groups in one person. It is likely that rich businessmen would have been Republicans. A writing frame is provided on **Worksheet 28** to support students.

The second spread looks at the other side of the opposition to the New Deal. The **Activity** on page 113 is a matching exercise to help students pin down some of the key points of the main opposition groups. **Worksheet 29** provides a chart on which students can record the main criticisms of the New Deal. This chart could be introduced at the beginning of the enquiry and students could fill it in as they work their way through.

Enquiry: The Supreme Court and the New Deal

Students' Book pp. 114–115

This enquiry looks at the conflict between Roosevelt and the Supreme Court. Again there is a focus on political cartoons as a means of examining the issues. It was this attempt by Roosevelt to pack the Supreme Court which led many Americans to be concerned that FDR was turning into some sort of dictator. Congress resisted him strongly, a clear example of the checks and balances of the Constitution in action.

CHAPTER 10: HOW SUCCESSFUL WAS THE NEW DEAL?

Teachers might like to consider this whole chapter for examination coursework since it provides opportunities to access a variety of assessment objectives. It could build towards a major activity requiring students to select and deploy information in a structured essay. Students could do preparatory work in groups or as a whole class and then be set individual assignments.

A genuine assessment of the New Deal at this level is very difficult as students find it hard to grasp the complexity of the total legislation programme. In the three spreads here, we have tried to show how it was successful in some ways and not in others, and how the experience of the New Deal varied a great deal over the USA.

Enquiry: Overview – what did the New Deal achieve?

Student's Book pp. 116–117
Worksheets 30, 31

The overview is designed to help students reach a general assessment of the New Deal. It brings to the fore the question of whether the New Deal brought economic recovery. It then goes on to look at historians' views about who the New Deal helped and what its overall value was. The conclusions for students remain open but they are most likely to follow the line that the New Deal, while not bringing full recovery and failing in certain areas, did help a great many people, left much of lasting value and had a profound impact on American politics.

The questions encourage students to look back over the section on the New Deal measures to collect evidence of other achievements and areas in which the New Deal helped people. This may best be done by using the grid on page 122. This encourages students to rate the aims of the New Deal on a scale. This is intended to make them understand that parts of the New Deal worked to a greater or a lesser extent. A copy of this grid can be found on **Worksheet 30**.

Worksheet 31 provides an example of conflicting evidence about how one agency, the NRA, worked. This would make a good homework or revision task requiring students to practise their skills of source evaluation. Spivak, from a left-wing stance, was collecting evidence to use to attack the New Deal, whereas Perkins was seeking to defend it. She, of course, was in Roosevelt's cabinet and therefore had a vested interest in defending the New Deal.

Enquiry: Did the New Deal reforms make life better for all Americans?

Students' Book pp. 118–119

This spread provides an overview of three main groups which have been tracked throughout the book – blacks, Native Americans and women. Other groups – sharecroppers, Mexicans, Latin-Americans – are mentioned briefly on the previous spread, but it would be impossible to deal with these in any depth. It is important, however, to point out that these groups did tend to suffer much more that those in mainstream white society and generally got less out of the New Deal.

Enquiry: Did the New Deal help labour unions?

Students' Book pp. 120–121

The unions had taken a bashing under the Republican Presidents in the 1920s. The New Deal gave workers the backing they needed to press employers to recognise unions in key industries. The employers resisted and there were violent confrontations throughout the 1930s.

THE USA BETWEEN THE WARS   STUDENTS' BOOK P. 122

Questions **5** and **6** ask students to think about how different groups of people can create different versions of the same events.

Enquiry: Summing up the New Deal's success?

Students' Book p. 122
Worksheets 31, 32

Worksheet 31 provides a copy of the grid on page 122 of the textbook. This can be used to help students sum up the achievements of the New Deal before they attempt the **Activity** at the bottom of page 122.

Writing the essay

This is an important essay in which students have to pull a number of different strands together. To help them do this, a full-scale supporting activity has been provided on **Worksheet 32**. This activity helps students to distinguish main points from supporting evidence or explantion. Students have to select the main points first and then find the supporting points that fit these.

Teachers will have to decide how much of this they need to use, depending on the ability and essay-writing skills of their students. Some might just want to use the main points and get students to brainstorm or develop for themselves the supporting points. Others might want students to do the full activity and then leave them to deploy the information themselves. Some students will need help in structuring the essay and deploying the information.

Running the activity

- Arrange students in pairs or small groups.
- Give each pair or group a set of cards which have been cut up, jumbled up. Tell them to spread out the cards on the table (desk) in front of them.
- Ask students to decide what the main points are (see below). Help any groups which are having difficulty.
- Tell students to put these points across the table to form a series of columns. Then ask them to sort the other cards into the columns by deciding which of the main points they support or explain, i.e. the main point should be at the top of the column and the supporting points underneath. The columns do not have to contain the same number of points.
- Students can add their own points or ideas. They can then use these columns to structure their essay.

The main points are:

- The New Deal did not bring full economic recovery
- The New Deal did help the economy and businesses
- The New Deal helped farmers and workers in trade unions
- The New deal helped a lot of people get through the Depression
- There were a lot of groups that did not do too well out of the New Deal
- The New Deal produced results of lasting value.

Enquiry: Was Franklin D. Roosevelt good for America in the 1930s?

Students' Book pp. 123–125
Worksheet 33

This enquiry considers different interpretations of Roosevelt's achievements at the end of the 1930s before judgements of him were coloured by his performance in the Second World War. Teachers could make this exercise simpler by cutting down the number of sources their students have to consider.

The **Activity** on page 125 is intended to make students use information selectively to present a particular case. **Worksheet 33** provides a writing frame to help students do this. Persuade some students to present the case against Roosevelt (this is more difficult). The pros and cons of Roosevelt's presidency in the 1930s can then be debated in class. Students could do preparatory work in groups, then produce their own written responses for assessment.

WORKSHEET 1

Coming to America

Use this worksheet to help you with the task on page 6. Some of the answers have been started for you. You can invent the family, where they came from and their hopes and expectations in the New World. Pages 7–9 in the textbook will help you do this.

Question: How did you feel at the end of your journey?

Answer: I cannot tell you how happy I felt as our ship entered New York harbour. We had …

Question: What were your feelings when you were taken to Ellis Island?

Answer: We did not really know what was going on. We were led …

… became very worried when we found out that we might not be allowed in …

Question: What was it like in the Great Hall?

Answer: We were put in long rows …

Question: What were the medical tests and registration questions like?

Answer: These were the worst thing. We were taken to inspection rooms where …

Our sister looked very ill, so …

Question: What were your main hopes and fears for the future?

Answer: We were so excited when we left the island. This was our chance …

© JOHN MURRAY   *The USA between the Wars Teachers' Resource Book*   25

WORKSHEET 2

Map of the USA

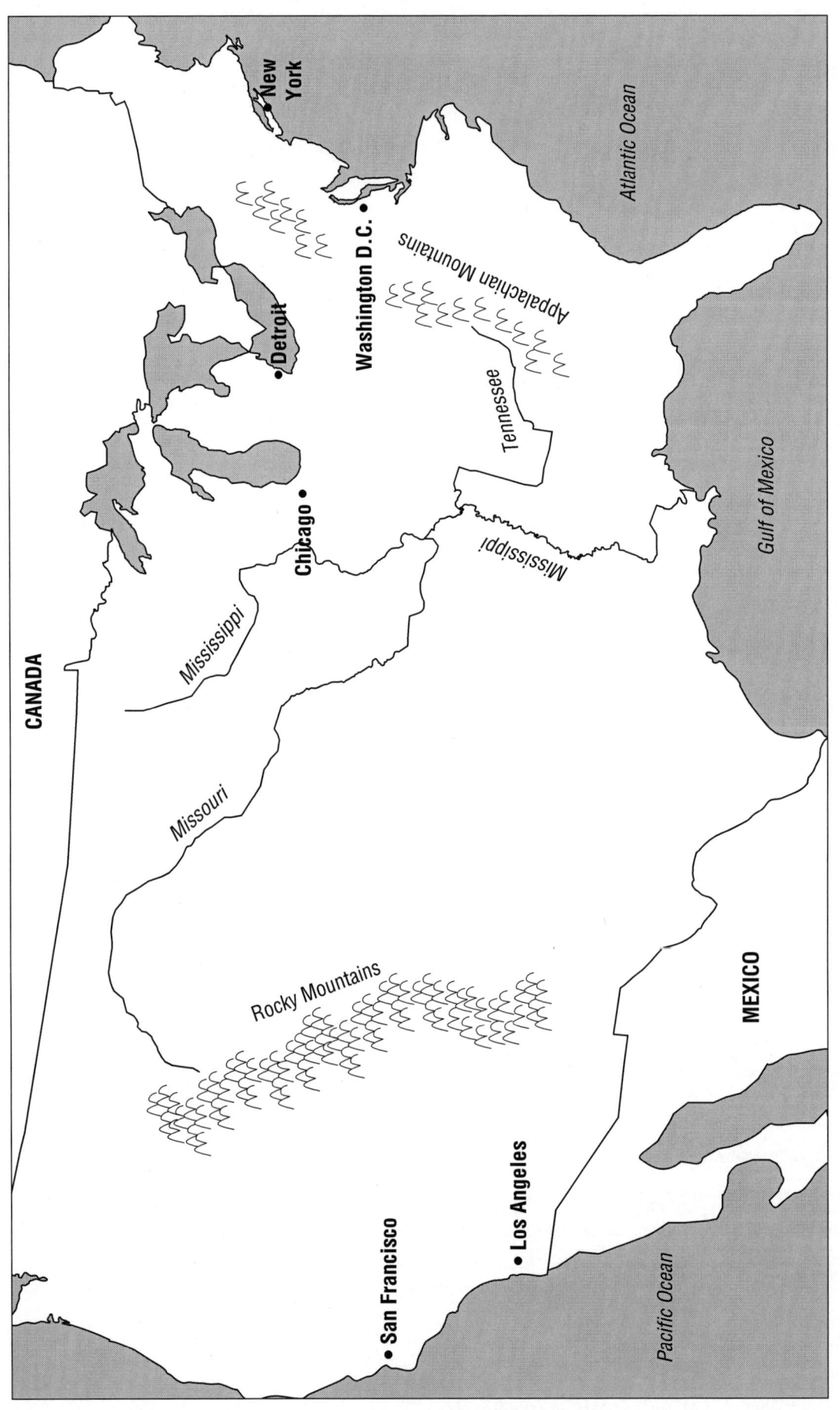

WORKSHEET 3

The government of the USA

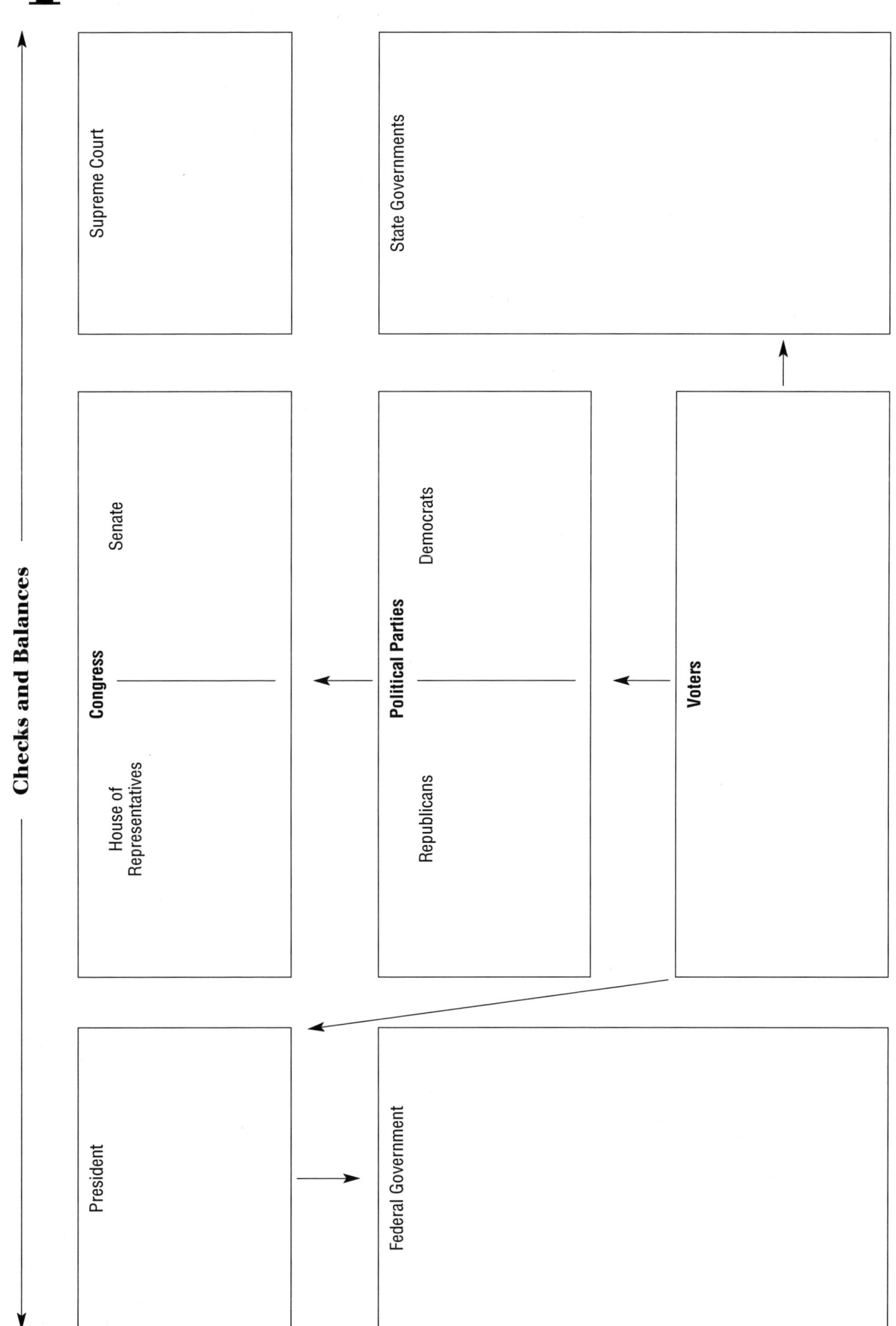

WORKSHEET 4
Two Republican Presidents

Warren Harding

Warren Harding was President of the USA from 1921 to 1923. Many people believe he was the least effective President ever elected by the American people. Harding said of himself that he was 'a man of limited talents from a small town'. He was, however, very popular with the voters, seen as a handsome, lovable and charming politician.

Harding ushered in the Republican pro-business policies of non-interference. Government controls on large business corporations were taken away and taxes were reduced. The 1920s' boom was under way. However, Harding's administration soon ran into difficulties. He had brought many of his old friends from Ohio into the government and they were corrupt, taking enormous bribes for favours. This led to a series of scandals. The worst was the Teapot Dome scandal where Albert Fall, the Secretary of the Interior, accepted huge bribes for allowing a private oil company to take oil intended as a reserve supply for the Navy.

Fortunately for Harding, he died of a sudden heart attack in 1923 before all the scandals came out into the open. Harding was clearly not up to the job of president. He liked the good life: he drank bootleg liquor, chewed tobacco and played poker with his Ohio friends. He pursued young women, enjoying sexual adventures away from his forbidding wife, whom he called the 'Duchess'.

Calvin Coolidge

Calvin Coolidge, Harding's Vice President, was sworn in as President in the middle of one night in August 1923. He remained President until 1929. He was just what the Republicans needed. He was upright, honest and a man of integrity. He was able to sort out the financial scandals without any real damage to the Republican Party.

Coolidge believed wholeheartedly in free enterprise. He went further than Harding in removing controls on business and financial institutions and cutting taxes. He said, 'The chief business of the American people is business.' He vetoed bills from Congress trying to help farmers by keeping up farm prices. He supported the breaking of trade union power. He wanted to give business free reign.

He also believed in doing as little as possible. He was famous for insisting on twelve hours' sleep a night and an afternoon nap. He was a man of few words and this earned him the nickname 'Silent Cal'. One popular story about him concerned a dinner guest who bet Coolidge she could make him say three words. 'You lose,' he replied.

Americans were surprised when he did not run for President in 1928. Some people think he had had some warning about the impending Depression.

WORKSHEET 5
How could you become the President?

HARRY TRUMAN 1884–1972
President: 1945–53
Born: Missouri
Father: wealthy farmer
Religion: Protestant
Job before election: soldier, judge
Party: Democrat

GERALD FORD 1913–
President: 1974–77
Born: Nebraska
Father: wool dealer
Religion: Protestant
Job before election: football coach, lawyer
Party: Republican

DWIGHT EISENHOWER 1890–1969
President: 1953–61
Born: Texas
Father: mechanic
Religion: Protestant
Job before election: general in the army
Party: Republican

JAMES CARTER 1924–
President: 1977–81
Born: Georgia
Father: farmer/businessman
Religion: Protestant
Job before election: peanut farmer
Party: Democrat

JOHN KENNEDY 1917–1963
President: 1961–63
Born: Massachusetts
Father: millionaire businessman
Religion: Catholic
Job before election: naval officer, journalist
Party: Democrat

RONALD REAGAN 1911–
President: 1981–89
Born: Illinois
Father: shoe salesman
Religion: Protestant
Job before election: actor
Party: Republican

LYNDON JOHNSON 1908–1973
President: 1963–69
Born: Texas
Father: farmer/local politician
Religion: Protestant
Job before election: teacher, secretary to a Congressman
Party: Democrat

GEORGE BUSH 1924–
President: 1989–93
Born: Massachusetts
Father: senator/banker
Religion: Protestant
Job before election: pilot and businessman
Party: Republican

RICHARD NIXON 1913–1994
President: 1969–74
Born: California
Father: lemon farmer
Religion: Protestant
Job before election: lawyer
Party: Republican

WILLIAM CLINTON 1946–
President: 1993–
Born: Arkansas
Father: car dealer
Religion: Protestant
Job before election: lawyer, politician
Party: Democrat

WORKSHEET 6

The boom in the 1920s

Use this chart to summarise how the products of the boom made life different in the 1920s.

Item	How this changed life in the 1920s
Cars	
Electricity in homes	
Electrical products such as vacuum cleaners, washing machines and refrigerators	
Radio	
Advertising	
Mail-order catalogues	
New cheap fabrics like rayon	
Big stores in cities	
Magazines	

WORKSHEET 7
What were the main features of the boom?

Use the diagram below as the starting point to draw a chart showing the main features of the boom and how they were linked to each other.

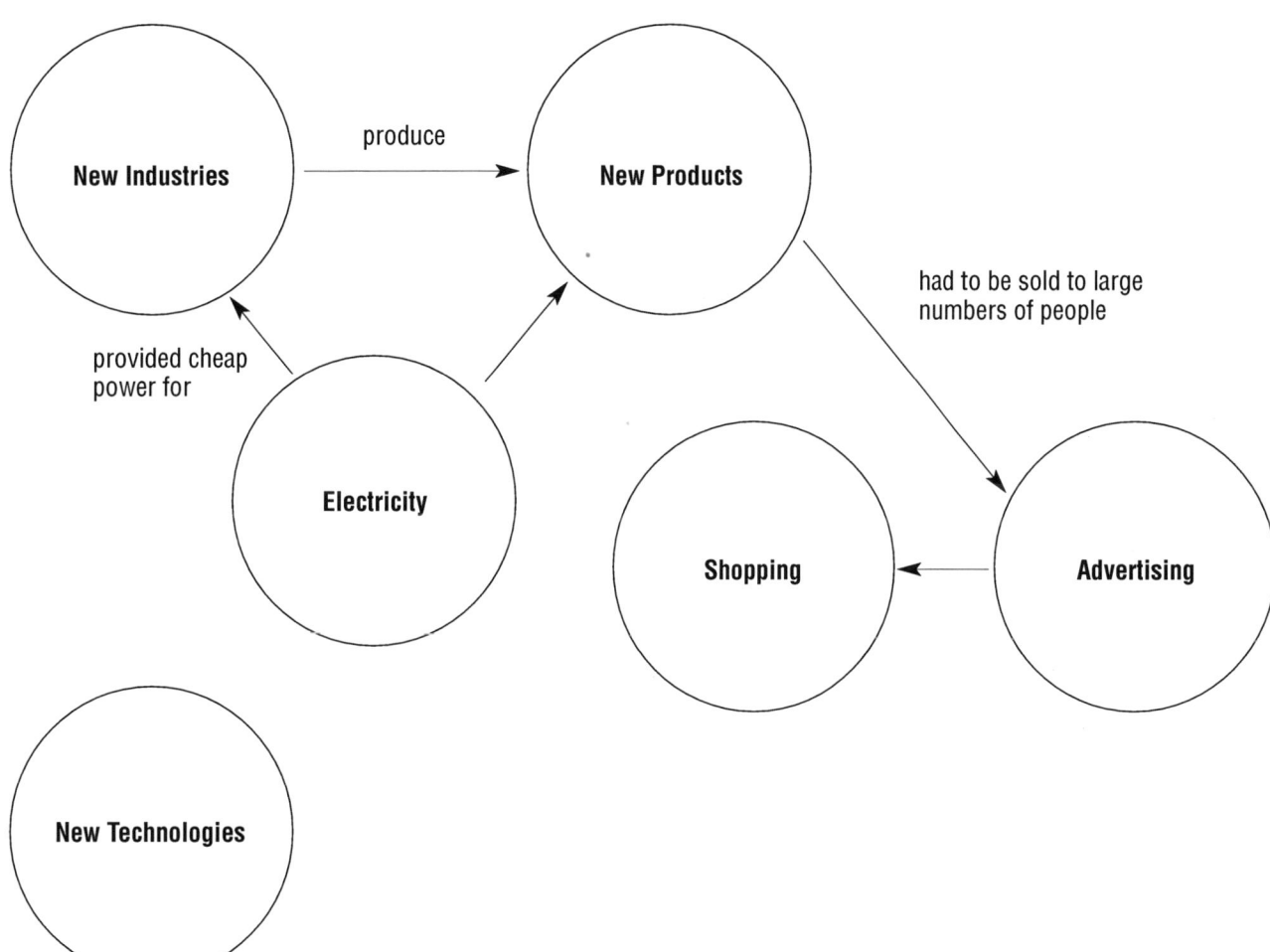

© JOHN MURRAY *The USA between the Wars Teachers' Resource Book*

WORKSHEET 8

The causes of the boom in the 1920s

Cut up the cards and give a set to each pair or group of students.

CONFIDENCE meant that Americans were willing to invest in new products and new ideas, and take risks.

The **MOTOR CAR** had a huge impact on the US economy. Thousands of people were employed making cars. It stimulated growth in other industries (metal, glass, rubber etc.) and in construction (road-building and house-building in the new suburbs).

NEW TECHNOLOGIES meant that new products could be developed, particularly ones which used plastic and synthetic fibres like rayon. The development of better ways of making and transporting electricity to people's homes meant they could use new electrical goods.

NATURAL RESOURCES – the USA had a great store of resources to power industry and provide raw materials for new industries.

MASS PRODUCTION TECHNIQUES meant that goods could be produced cheaply in huge quantities. This made them affordable for ordinary Americans.

CREDIT allowed many more Americans to buy goods even if they did not have the money immediately available. This kept up demand for industrial products.

ADVERTISING, CHAIN STORES and BIG MAIL-ORDER COMPANIES helped to ensure the mass consumption of goods. Enormous numbers of people had to buy the new goods to keep the boom going.

The **FIRST WORLD WAR** gave American industry a flying start in the 1920s. US industries had grown during the war and were geared up ready to meet the enormous demand for US goods when the war ended.

The **POLICIES OF THE REPUBLICAN PRESIDENTS** were pro-business. Restrictions and regulations were removed to help businesses expand. Taxes were lowered to give people more money to spend.

WORKSHEET 9
Why was there a boom in the USA in the 1920s?

Use the ideas below to help you write your essay.

Paragraph 1
In the 1920s, the USA was booming. Businesses grew, people became wealthy, new buildings were constructed and thousands of miles of roads were laid. Americans were able to buy a whole range of new products like cars, radios and washing machines. Why did the US economy grow so fast at this time? Historians have suggested that a number of factors worked together to cause the boom.

Paragraph 2
The most important reason for the boom was ...

Paragraph 3
Other important factors which helped bring the boom about were ...

Paragraph 4
Factors which contributed to the boom were ...

Paragraph 5
(In your conclusion, explain how the factors were linked to each other and depended on each other.)

WORKSHEET 10A

Would you have made a good Republican president in the 1920s?

> You are going to see if you would have made the same decisions as the Republican Presidents about important issues in the 1920s.
>
> Make sure you have read page 28 of the text book before you do do this exercise.

1. It is the early 1920s. Farmers are producing too much food. Prices are falling and farmers are going bankrupt.
   Should President Coolidge:
   a) let the farmers sort out their own problems ☐
   b) use government money to buy surplus produce to keep farm prices at a reasonable level ☐
   c) appoint a government official to plan how much food farmers should produce. ☐

2. Low wages and dangerous working conditions have led to strikes in the coal and textile industries. Employers have used armed guards to break the strikes.
   Should President Coolidge:
   a) send officials to arrange talks between the two sides and try to make the employers be more reasonable ☐
   b) support the trades unions and put pressure on the employers to raise wages to a fair level ☐
   c) support the employers and encourage state governments to use police to end the strikes. ☐

3. Some States want to ban the use of child labour and fix a minimum wage for women workers because their wages are so low.
   Should President Coolidge:
   a) support measures to ban child labour and fix minimum wages for women ☐
   b) do nothing at all about these issues ☐
   c) encourage employers to pay women higher wages and not to employ children. ☐

4. During the First World War, the USA lent European countries millions of dollars. These countries are too poor to pay their debts and cannot afford to buy American goods. However, they want to sell their goods in the USA.
   Should President Harding:
   a) help European countries to sell their goods in the USA so that world trade improves ☐
   b) put tariffs (a type of tax) on European goods coming into the USA so that Americans buy American goods which would be cheaper ☐
   c) give more loans to Europe so that they can buy American goods. ☐

5. In the early 1920s, there are social problems, including violence and high levels of crime, in many of the northern cities. One reason for this is the large number of immigrants who arrived in the USA between 1900 and 1914.
   Should President Harding:
   a) stop immigration completely ☐
   b) allow immigration to continue at a slightly reduced rate and give government money to help immigrants living in ghettos ☐
   c) cut immigration and allow in only immigrants from northern Europe who are regarded as 'higher quality' newcomers. ☐

6. During the war, the government owned and operated huge dams on the Tennessee River at Muscle Shoals to generate power to produce explosives. In the 1920s, Senator Norris wants the government to operate these dams to produce cheap electricity for the poor people of the Tennessee Valley.
   Should President Coolidge:
   a) support Senator Norris ☐
   b) allow the government to compete with private companies in the electricty industry ☐
   c) stop any plans for the government to produce electricity in competition with private companies. ☐

7. Throughout the 1920s, religious groups in America have attacked the amount of sex in cinema films. A series of sex and drugs scandals involving Hollywood film stars have led to demands for censorship.
   Should President Coolidge:
   a) bring in strict censorship laws to control sex scenes in films ☐
   b) let the film industry set up its own scheme to maintain moral standards ☐
   c) do nothing at all. ☐

WORKSHEET 10B

Answers: Would you have made a good Republican president in the 1920s?

The answers below show the actions taken by the Republican Presidents in the 1920s. You score 3 points for every decision you made which agrees with their actions. Add up your score at the end and compare it with the table below.

Under 9
Low score – you disagree with the actions the Republican Presidents took. It does not necessarily mean that you would have made a bad president. Some of your decisions would have helped a lot of poor Americans in the 1920s.

9–12
Medium score – you agree with some of the actions they took.

15–21
High score – you would have made a brilliant Republican president. You agree with the courses of action they took.

Answers
The letter shows the answer which agrees with the action taken by Republican Presidents in the 1920s.

1. a)
President Coolidge vetoed several Bills from Congress on farm prices. Congressmen tried to find ways to keep farm prices up, e.g. buying up surplus produce to stop prices falling. But the Republicans would not intervene because of their policy of non-interference. As a result, farmers becoming increasingly poor throughout the 1920s.

2. c)
The Republicans were on the side of big business. They wanted to break the power of the unions. They supported employers who would only employ non-union labour. State governors, encouraged by the Republicans, used state troopers to break several strikes.

3. b)
The Republican Presidents did nothing about these issues following their policy of non-interference in business. The Supreme Court, dominated by Republican judges, declared that laws designed to stop child labour in industries were unconstitutional. The Court also banned laws setting down minimum wages for women.

4. b)
The US government was annoyed with European countries because they could not pay their debts. They wanted to protect US industry and encourage Americans to buy American-made goods. So, in 1922 the Fordney–McCumber Act put tariffs on European goods coming into the USA, making them more expensive. European countries retaliated by putting tariffs on American goods. As a result international trade slumped.

5. c)
The Republicans brought in restrictions on the number of immigrants allowed in, particularly those whom they regarded as the cause of problems in the cities, e.g. southern and eastern Europeans. See page 46 of the textbook.

6. c)
Coolidge vetoed a bill providing for government operation of the dams. The Republicans believed that it was wrong for the government to compete with private companies. Some Republicans wanted to sell the dams to private companies.

7. b)
The government was under pressure to bring in laws but was reluctant to get involved. It was therefore happy to support the film industry's own effort – the Hay's code – which controlled nudity and the length of kisses on screen, and ensured that films did not support crime or wrong-doing.

WORKSHEET 11
Would you have wanted to work for Henry Ford?

Henry Ford paid his workers much more than most other industrial workers but he made them earn their wages. Anybody who complained or caused any trouble was sacked. Yet he also had a paternalistic (fatherly) attitude towards his workers. He set up a special department to look after them. Department staff visited their homes to teach them about clean and healthy living. He set up classes in English (many of the workers were immigrants) and other subjects to help them better themselves.

SOURCE 1 E.G. Pipp, editor of Ford's newspaper, *The Deerbourne Gazette*, was close to Ford. But they later fell out and Pipp wrote a book about the way Ford operated.

❝ One day Ford said he was going to cut the price of the car in an amount nearly equal to the profit.
'How are you going to get your profit?' I asked.
'I am going to make them dig for it,' he said and set his jaws tight.
The cut was made in price and it was followed up with a speeding up in the factory that was felt all over the plant. The assembly line was made to move faster, so some men who had been operating one machine were made to operate two ...

... Anyone riding in a street car about the time there is a shift leaving the Ford plant, must be impressed with the exhausted condition of the men. One sees many of them so exhausted they scarcely hold up their heads, many are scarcely seated before they are asleep. Keeping up with the machinery to which their every motion must be timed and having that machine speeded up more and more takes the energy out of the men and produces more cars for Ford. ❞

SOURCE 2 John Dos Passos, *USA*, 1936

❝ Ford's production was improving all the time; less waste, more spotters, stoolpigeons (fifteen minutes for lunch, three minutes to go to the toilet, the Taylorised speed up everywhere, reachunder, adjustwasher, screwdown bolt, shove in cotterpin, reachunder, adjustwasher, screwdown bolt, reachunderadjustscrewdownreachunderadjust, until every ounce of life was sucked off into production and at night the workmen went home gray shaking husks. ❞

SOURCE 3 A worker at a Ford car factory describes his feeling about his work

❝ People often say to me: 'Bud, what is it like to work for old Henry Ford?' And I tell them: 'That was the word for it – W.O.R.K spelled work.' You didn't do anything else all the time you were there. It wasn't a longer working day than in other jobs. It just seemed long, because there was no let up ... Each man on the line had one job to do, and that was all. I remember once, all I had to do was tighten one nut ... And they had that line moving so fast there was only enough time to make sure the nut was good and tight before the chassis moved on.
Monotonous? Well, I guess it was. It seemed to suit some of the gang: they didn't want to think about what they were doing ... The pay? That wasn't bad, but we sure earned it ... ❞

1. What impression do Sources 1–3 give you about:
■ Ford's attitude to work
■ the effects of his way of working on the factory workers.

2. Do you think John Dos Passos (Source 2) was a fan of Henry Ford's methods of working? Explain your answer.

3. How did Ford help his workers? What do you think about the way he did this?

4. What would have been the good and bad things about working for Henry Ford?

WORKSHEET 12
The significance of Henry Ford

Cut up cards and give a set to each pair or group of students.

Ford was a mechanical genius. He designed the Model T Ford with interchangeable parts and unique rear springs which meant it could travel over rough ground more easily.

Ford was the first person to develop the techniques of assembly-line production using conveyor belts and mechanical devices which allowed large volumes of goods to be produced much more cheaply.

Ford's ideas about mass production were copied across the USA. Huge amounts of cheap products appeared on the market which ordinary Americans could afford.

Ford made cars affordable for millions of ordinary Americans. He forced the prices of cars down because he wanted more people to own them, as well as making a lot of money for himself.

The Model T Ford changed the face of America (roads, suburbs, petrol stations etc.) and the way people lived their lives. It gave immense freedom to the people who lived in the countryside.

Ford had an excellent business sense which made his company successful. In particular, he understood that you could make a good profit by selling more cars cheaply instead of a few more expensively.

Ford raised the wages of his men to $5 a day to attract workers and stop them leaving his plants. This was much higher than what other companies were paying.

Henry Ford had great drive and determination. Even though he had problems, he never gave up and was determined to succeed.

Ford did a lot of harm to the Jewish community. His anti-Semitic articles gave support to intolerant anti-Jewish fanatics in the Ku Klux Klan and similar organisations.

Ford used a system of informers to root out trade-union sympathisers and hired thugs to beat them up. This encouraged other companies to use violent strong-arm tactics against union members.

Ford built the Greenfield Museum which is is full of American historical objects, even whole houses. It presents a unique view of American history and is visited by millions of people.

Ford gave millions of dollars to charity. He supported a hospital and an orphanage.

© JOHN MURRAY   *The USA between the Wars* Teachers' Resource Book

WORKSHEET 13

Why is Henry Ford significant in American history?

Use the ideas below to help you write your essay.

Henry Ford was the pioneer of mass production
(Explain what this is, how other companies copied him and why this is important.)

Henry Ford was a mechanical genius
(Write about how he developed the Model T and mechanical systems for the assembly line.)

Henry Ford made cars affordable
(Explain why this was significant.)

The Model T had a huge impact on America
(Describe and explain.)

Ford is also significant in American history for other reasons
(Describe and explain these.)

WORKSHEET 14

Who didn't benefit from the boom?

Make notes in the boxes below to explain why the different groups did not benefit from the boom.

Black People

New Immigrants

Farmers

Industrial Workers

© JOHN MURRAY *The USA between the Wars Teachers' Resource Book* 39

WORKSHEET 15
The Red Scare

Look at the cartoon on the right:

1. What is the man in the foreground doing?

2. Who do you think the weeds represent? (Clue: label attached to basket.)

3. What is the woman in the background sowing?

4. What is the message of the cartoon?

Give the American Bluegrass a show
(Cartoonist Ding in the New York *Tribune*)

Look at the cartoon on the left:

5. What is happening in the background? (Who do the characters represent?)

6. Who is standing in the foreground?

7. Why is he not doing anything to help?

8. What is the message of the cartoon?

9. Why do you think these cartoons appeared in newspapers during the Red Scare?

Strikers
(Cartoonist Gale in the Los Angeles *Times*)

40   *The USA between the Wars* Teachers' Resource Book   © JOHN MURRAY

WORKSHEET 16

Rough justice for Sacco and Vanzetti

Prepare notes for a script for a TV programme which is looking back at the trial of Sacco and Vanzetti. The producer wants to show that this was a famous case of injustice based on prejudice. Write your notes in the boxes below.

BOX 1

Explain the background to the trial (including the Red Scare).

BOX 2

Describe the conflicting evidence in the trial. Remember that your programme has a bias in favour of Sacco and Vanzetti.

BOX 3

Focus on the judge

BOX 4

Look at how the verdict was given and Vanzetti's last statement at the trial.

BOX 5

Draw conclusions about the trial and why the two men were found guilty.

© JOHN MURRAY *The USA between the Wars Teachers' Resource Book* 41

WORKSHEET 17
The Ku Klux Klan

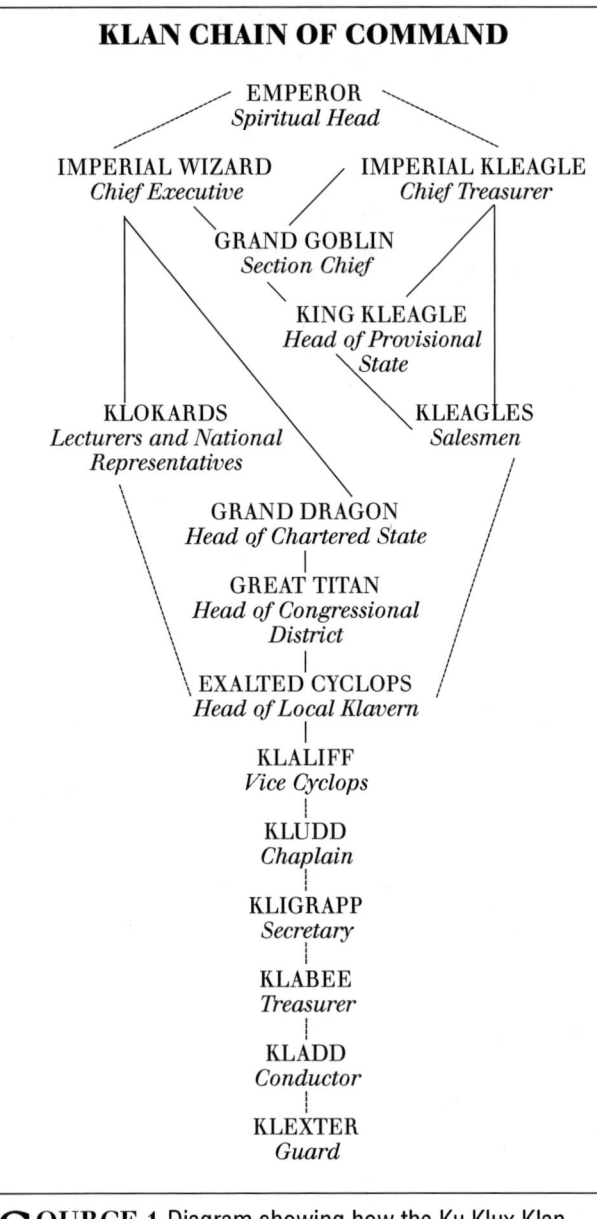

KLAN CHAIN OF COMMAND

EMPEROR
Spiritual Head

IMPERIAL WIZARD
Chief Executive

IMPERIAL KLEAGLE
Chief Treasurer

GRAND GOBLIN
Section Chief

KING KLEAGLE
Head of Provisional State

KLOKARDS
Lecturers and National Representatives

KLEAGLES
Salesmen

GRAND DRAGON
Head of Chartered State

GREAT TITAN
Head of Congressional District

EXALTED CYCLOPS
Head of Local Klavern

KLALIFF
Vice Cyclops

KLUDD
Chaplain

KLIGRAPP
Secretary

KLABEE
Treasurer

KLADD
Conductor

KLEXTER
Guard

SOURCE 1 Diagram showing how the Ku Klux Klan was organised.

SOURCE 2 Colonel Winfield Jones, *Story of the Ku Klux Klan*, 1921, quotes a statement from a Klan leader

" We are not anti-Jewish; a Jew who can subscribe to the tenets of the Christian Religion can get in. We are not anti-negro. Scores of other fraternal organizations do not admit negroes. We are not anti-foreign born, we merely require that members be native born Americans.

The Knights of the Ku Klux Klan is a purely patriotic fraternal organization ... It stands for the preservation of American ideals and institutions, the protection of the home, the chastity of womanhood, the maintenance of the blood-bought rights and liberties of the Anglo-Saxon race ... The Ku Klux Klan stands unreservedly and unashamedly for white supremacy in America. "

1. Why do you think the Klan used the strange set of names in Source 1?

_____
_____
_____
_____

2. What do sources 2 and 3 tell you about the aims and membership of the Ku Klux Klan?

_____
_____
_____
_____

FORM K-115

APPLICATION FOR CITIZENSHIP
IN THE
INVISIBLE EMPIRE
Knights of the Ku Klux Klan
(INCORPORATED)

To *His Majesty the Imperial Wizard, Emperor of the Invisible Empire, Knights of the Ku Klux Klan:*

I, the undersigned, a native born, true and loyal citizen of the United States of America, being a white male Gentile person of temperate habits, sound in mind and a believer in the tenets of the Christian religion, the maintenance of White Supremacy and the principles of "pure Americanism," do most respectfully apply for membership in the Knights of the Klu Klux Klan through Klan No._____, Realm of_____

I guarantee on my honor to confirm strictly to all rules and requirements regulating my "naturalization" and the continuance of my membership, and at all times a strict and loyal obedience to your constitutional authority and the constitution and laws of the fraternity, not in conflict with the constitution and constitutional laws of the United States of America and the states thereof. If I prove untrue as a Klansman I will willingly accept as my portion whatever penalty your authority may impose.

The required "klectokon" accompanies this application.

Signed _____ Applicant

Endorsed by
Kl_____   Residence Address _____
Kl_____   Business Address _____
                                Date _____, 192____

The person securing this application must sign on top line above.   NOTICE—Check the address to which mail may be sent.

SOURCE 3 Application form for the Klan, 1921

WORKSHEET 18
The Rosewood incident

At the end of 1922, the village of Rosewood in Florida was doing well. It had its own school, three churches and a railway station. The population of Rosewood were almost entirely black. Most farmed or worked in the nearby mill town of Sumner. By the end of January 1923, Rosewood no longer existed and the people who had lived there had disappeared. How did this happen?

On January 1, 1923, a white woman called Fannie Taylor ran out of her house in Sumner screaming that she had been attacked, some say raped, by a black man. Suspicion fell on an escaped black convict, Jesse Hunter. A posse was formed, dogs were brought in and the hunt was on. The dogs led the posse to Rosewood.

The trail led to the house of the blacksmith, Sam Carter. He was pulled out of the house, tortured into confessing he had helped the convict to escape, and hanged from a tree. But Jesse Hunter was not found.

Over the following days, whites gathered in Sumner and there was talk of an armed raid on Rosewood to find Hunter, although there was no proof that he was there. Sylvester Carrier, a prominent figure in the Rosewood black community, made it clear he would defend his family against attack and gathered a number of blacks together in his home.

The white mob saw this as a challenge, went to Carrier's home and tried to break in. A gunfight started and two white men were shot dead. Sarah Carrier, Sylvester's mother, called on the mob to go home, but she was shot and killed. The shooting restarted and a siege of the house went on for several hours. During the night, most of the people in the house escaped. In daylight, the attackers broke in, finding only the bodies of Sylvester Carrier and his mother. They burnt the house to the ground.

But the mob were not finished with Rosewood. They turned their attention to other buildings in the village. They burnt the church and five more houses. The terrified villagers fled into the woods and swamps nearby. Some were killed or wounded trying to escape.

The state authorities knew what was going on but did nothing to help. On Sunday, January 7, the mob returned to burn the last houses in Rosewood. The village had been wiped out – except for one house, a house in which white people lived. Unbeknown to the mob, the man who lived in this house, Jim Wright, was sheltering several of his black neighbours.

It is not known how many people died during the Rosewood riots. Whole families just disappeared and were not heard of again. Many escaped by rail, helped by two white railroad workers. The whole incident was buried, that is, until a few years ago.

A reporter stumbled on the story and it became frontpage news. Survivors told of the events of that horrendous week in January and lawyers took the state of Florida to court seeking compensation. In 1994, they were awarded $2 million dollars.

Rosewood is significant in several ways. It was one of the rare instances during the 1920s when a black community fought back, which is no doubt one of the reasons why the mob destroyed it completely. It seems that Rosewood's white neighbours did not like to see a black community doing well. There was no connection between Rosewood and the attack on Fannie Taylor: later evidence points to her being beaten up by her white lover. It is also significant that the state authorities did nothing about it although they knew what was happening.

The Rosewood incident has reopened issues about race in the Southern states of America. In Florida, the present-day Ku Klux Klan is very strong and in recent years a large number of black churches have been burned down. It does not seem that the views and values of some people in the white community have changed much over the last seventy years.

TASK

Write two short paragraphs explaining:

- what the Rosewood incident tells us about white attitudes to black people in the Southern states of America in the 1920s

- why it is important to know about this today.

or

Write the news story about Rosewood as if you were the reporter who had uncovered the details of what had happened.

WORKSHEET 19
Two black leaders

Marcus Garvey

James Weldon Johnson

Marcus Garvey was born in Jamaica in 1887. He received only a basic education, leaving school to work as an apprentice. By the time he was 18, he was a master printer. He lost his job because he supported printing workers in a strike. He migrated to Central America where he was shocked by the exploitation of West Indian migrants.

In 1912, Garvey came to London where he met black intellectuals, discussed political ideas and began working as a radical journalist. In 1914, he returned to Jamaica to set up the Universal Negro Improvement Association (UNIA) to improve the position of negroes in Jamaica where they suffered discrimination at the hands of the whites who ruled the island. He wanted to create a sense of identity and pride in being black and encourage blacks to run their own affairs. But he could not get much support in Jamaica and so left for America in 1916.

Garvey set up UNIA in Harlem and his ideas soon proved attractive to poor black Americans. He encouraged Black Pride and blamed the misfortunes of black people on white racism. He set up a newspaper, *The Negro World*, and worked through organisations like churches, militant groups and trade unions. UNIA was extremely popular, with over a million members by 1921.

Garvey wanted blacks to be self-reliant and not dependent on the white world. He preached separatism. This led him to fall out with other black leaders who wanted integration with white society. Garvey stressed the cultural links between black Americans and Africans. He created the Black Star Shipping Company to carry migrants back to Africa where he hoped to set up a new African republic with himself as president. But the whole venture collapsed in financial chaos. Garvey was accused of fraud and put in prison. In 1927, he was deported to Jamaica.

James Weldon Johnson was born in Jacksonville, Florida, in 1871. His mother was a school teacher. Educated at Atlanta University, he developed his skills as a public speaker and a writer. He became principal of the grammar school he had attended and later one of the few black lawyers in Jacksonville. He also worked for the government as a consul in Venezuela.

In 1914, he joined the National Association for the Advancement of Coloured People (NAACP). He helped set up branches across America and in 1920 was made its leader. He helped turn it into an effective organisation. He put all his efforts into securing equal rights for blacks and ran a successful campaign against lynching.

Johnson also helped to shape the cultural movement known as the Harlem Renaissance. Johnson was a poet and a novelist, publishing in 1907 *The Autobiography of an Ex-Colored Man*, which examined racism in the Southern states of the USA. In the 1920s, he helped bring together and encourage the young black writers who came to Harlem in New York. He wanted to show how black artistic work had influenced American culture and make whites aware of the black experience in the USA. The Harlem Renaissance had a major impact on literature in America. In 1930, Johnson became Professor of Creative Writing at Fisk University.

WORKSHEET 20
Religious revival in the 1920s

Many Americans were were worried about the changes in social attitudes and values in the 1920s. Women wore short skirts and make-up, drank and smoked. People danced to the wild rhythms of black jazz music in night clubs. The cinema was spreading ideas of sexual freedom. These new values were associated with the cities where church attendance was declining.

Some people, particularly those who lived in small towns and in the countryside, looked to religion to fight these 'modern' values. There was a strong move back to old-style fundamentalist religion in an attempt to re-establish traditional Christian values in America.

Revivalists tried to inspire people to go back to church. One of the most famous was Billy Sunday. He worked in the South and used his sermons to attack dancing, gambling, foreigners, Communists and anyone who would not kiss the American flag. He became a public hero and a millionaire. Another was Aimée Semple McPherson. She raised one million dollars to build a temple in Los Angeles. It had a huge lighted cross on its top that could be seen for 50 miles. The Temple had seating for 5,000 people and they flocked to see her 'shows' (see **Source 2**).

Aimée Semple McPherson

SOURCE 1 Extract from a handbill given out by Pastor Albert H. Crombie in the town of Harvey, North Dakota, 1925

" NEXT SUNDAY NIGHT – AT 7.30 O'CLOCK SHARP, I AM GOING TO PREACH THE PLAINEST, STRAIGHTEST AND HOTTEST SERMON ABOUT THE SINS OF HARVEY THAT I KNOW HOW TO PREACH. Judge what it will be like by my sermons on dancing, card playing, movies and tobacco. I haven't room here to tell you much about it but if you want to know what my subject will be – here it is:
'UNDER THE LID OF HARVEY – THE SINS OF OUR CITY'
In that sermon I am going to tell you about the Officers and certain Citizens of our City and show you just what people believe is going on, such as home brewing – bootlegging, gambling – cigarette selling – and WORSE THINGS ... "

SOURCE 2 D. Wallechinsky and I. Wallace, *The People's Almanac*, 1975. A description of one of Sister Aimée's services

" There was always a good deal of pageantry in Aimée's services. In her 'Throw out the Lifeline' number, a dozen maidens clad in white clung desperately to a storm-lashed Rock of Ages, while special-effects men laboured mightily to create thunder, lightning and wind. Just when all seemed lost, out jumped Sister Aimée in an admiral's uniform to order a squad of lady sailors to the rescue. They tossed out the blessed lifeline, while the male chorus dressed as coastguardsmen, swept the mechanical waves with searchlights. The virgins were saved, trumpets blared and the congregation cheered while the American flag waved triumphantly over all. "

1. Why do you think so many Americans were turning to religion?

2. Thousands of Americans were attracted to the services of Billy Sunday, Sister Aimée and the preacher in Source 2. Explain why you think this was. Do you think their appeal was only religious?

WORKSHEET 21
Will you vote for Prohibition?

The following characters can be used for the Prohibition role-play.

1. A member of the Women's Christian Temperance Union. You believe that the only way to end the evils associated with alcohol is to ban its sale.

2. A male member of the Anti-Saloon League. You believe that the sale of alcohol should be restricted and saloons closed down because of the evils associated with them.

3. A high-society woman. You have become convinced before 1918 that many of the evils of society, especially crime and roblems in families, are the direct result of the consumption of alcohol. You want to stop these social evils.

4. A well-off man who enjoys a drink or two. But, before 1918, you are appalled by the crime and other social problems that appear to be connected with drinking alcohol. Reluctantly, you think something must be done to stop this.

5. A businessman who owns a small factory making clothes. You have been looking very closely at the arguments about banning the sale of alcohol. You are particularly thinking about how it might affect your workers. Your factory is in a run-down part of Chicago.

6. A worker in a car factory. You have always enjoyed regular drinking sessions with your friends. However, you are worried by all the posters you have seen showing what terrible effects alcohol can have on people's lives. You also think it might be unpatriotic to drink beer.

7. A farmer who lives in Ohio. You have a very strong religious background. You believe that life should be lived simply and that people should work hard. You believe that drinking alcohol is wrong.

8. A 32-year-old woman with two sons who live in Chicago. You would like this to be a pleasant place in which to live and bring up your children. In 1918, you are concerned about the social problems in the city, the drinking and the violence in the ghettos, and would like something to be done about these.

WORKSHEET 22

Why did Prohibition fail?

Use the ideas below to help you write the essay on page 63.

Many Americans did not really support Prohibition because …

It was very difficult to enforce Prohibition because …

The profits from selling illegal alcohol were so great that …

Important businessmen got involved in the trade. This meant that …

Prohibition was meant to decrease crime and lawlessness, but …

© JOHN MURRAY *The USA between the Wars Teachers' Resource Book*

WORKSHEET 23
Gangsters

Vincent 'Mad Dog' Coll

Born 1909, in the Irish ghetto of Hell's Kitchen, New York. Vince and his brother started as rum-runners and hired guns for Dutch Schultz. In 1931, Vince asked Dutch for a share in the bootlegging. When Dutch refused, Vince started hijacking his trucks, gang war broke out and Dutch's men shot Vince's brother in the street. Vince personally took care of four of the Schultz men.

On July 28 he tried to machine-gun down some of the Schultz henchmen in Spanish Harlem but hit five children in the street and killed a five-year-old. The public were outraged and Vince gave himself up. But not before he used some kidnap ransom money to hire top lawyer Sam Leibowitz who got him acquitted.

'Mad Dog' was bad for business and many of the racketeers wanted him out of the way. Three people were killed and two wounded when four gunmen hit a card game where Vince was tipped to be. Eight days later, on the February 9, 1932, Vince was sprayed with bullets from a machine gun as he was making a call from a drug store telephone booth. He was not yet 24.

Charles 'Lucky' Luciano

Born in 1897, Sicily. Soon after his arrival in the USA, Luciano started his own protection racket (at the age of 10). As a teenager, he joined the Five Points Gang with Capone and was soon suspected of many murders by the police. He worked his way up to be the chief henchman of Joe 'The Boss' Masseria who had built up the most powerful Mafia gang in New York.

Joe was an old-time Sicilian and would not deal with the Jewish gangs in New York. This annoyed his chief lieutenants, particularly 'Lucky' Luciano. To them, making money was more important than old Sicilian codes of honour. Luciano and others were secretly doing deals with the Jewish gangs. On 5 April, 1931, Luciano had Masseria killed. He was shot dead by four gunmen in the middle of a game of cards with Luciano. Luciano told police:

'I was in the can taking a leak. I always take a long leak.'

Luciano became number two in the powerful gang run by Maranzano, but soon had him killed too. Luciano was now the chief of the the American Mafia and was free to join up with Jewish, Irish, Polish and WASP gangs to form the National Crime Syndicate. The Syndicate had its own hired killers called Murder Incorporated. They were given 'contracts' to eliminate unwanted mobsters by the big gang bosses. Truly, this was 'organised' crime.

In 1936 Luciano was given 30–50 years in prison. He only served ten and continued to run the Syndicate from his cell. On his release, he was deported to Italy. He died from a heart attack in 1962 in Italy.

Harry 'Pittsburgh Phil' Strauss

Born 1908, Brooklyn, New York. Phil was the top hit man for Murder Incorporated. Mobs and crime families out of New York would ask for him specially. If one of the big gangsters suspected someone of informing, Phil would get the contract. He was linked by the police to 58 murders but it is likely that he killed well over a hundred people. This was more than any of the other top guns for Murder Incorporated such as Vito 'Chicken Head' Gurino, 'Blue Jaw' Magoon or Frank 'the Dasher' Abbandando.

Phil was a daring killer. He shot Harry Millman dead in a crowded restaurant (wounding five other diners) and then strolled out. In 1940 one of the bosses of Murder Incorporated, Abe 'Kid Twist' Reles started talking. He informed on the whole outfit before going out of a sixth-floor window while under police protection. The evidence was so solid Phil decided to plead insanity. He would not wash, shave or change his clothes. He spent most of the trial trying to eat his lawyer's briefcase. It did Phil no good. On June 12, 1941, he died in the electric chair.

WORKSHEET 23 (continued)

1. Draw a chart like the one below. Fill in the chart using the information on this worksheet and on Al Capone (pages 64–65 in the textbook).

Name	Ethnic origin	How became a gangster	How became powerful	How died
Vincent Coll				
Charles Luciano				
Harry Strauss				
Al Capone				

2. What are the similarities in the backgrounds of the gangsters?

_____
_____

3. What are the similarities in the way they rose to power (how they started off and the methods they used)?

_____
_____

4 a) The gangsters have been called 'ghetto criminals'. What do you think this means?

_____
_____

b) Why might the ghettos have produced more than their fair share of criminals?

_____
_____

5. What conclusions can you draw about:

■ the reasons for the rise of the gangsters in the 1920s

_____
_____

■ why they became so powerful?

_____
_____

© JOHN MURRAY   *The USA between the Wars   Teachers' Resource Book*

WORKSHEET 24
What were the causes of the Wall Street Crash?

1. Explain how the factors below contributed to the Wall Street Crash.

Factor	How it helped cause the Crash
Overproduction in American industry	
Wealth of 1920s not evenly distributed – a very large number of poor Americans	
Restricted market for US goods in other countries	
Speculators playing the market with borrowed money	
Panic selling of shares in October 1929	

2. What do you think was the most important cause of the Crash? Explain your answer.

_____
_____
_____
_____
_____

WORKSHEET 25

Black people in the Depression

SOURCE 1 William Siegel, 'Civilised America'. The Depression increased racial tensions. Lynchings rose from 7 in 1921 to 21 in 1930 and 28 in 1933. In 1934, Claude Neal was cut into pieces by a mob and his mutilated limbs were hung from a tree

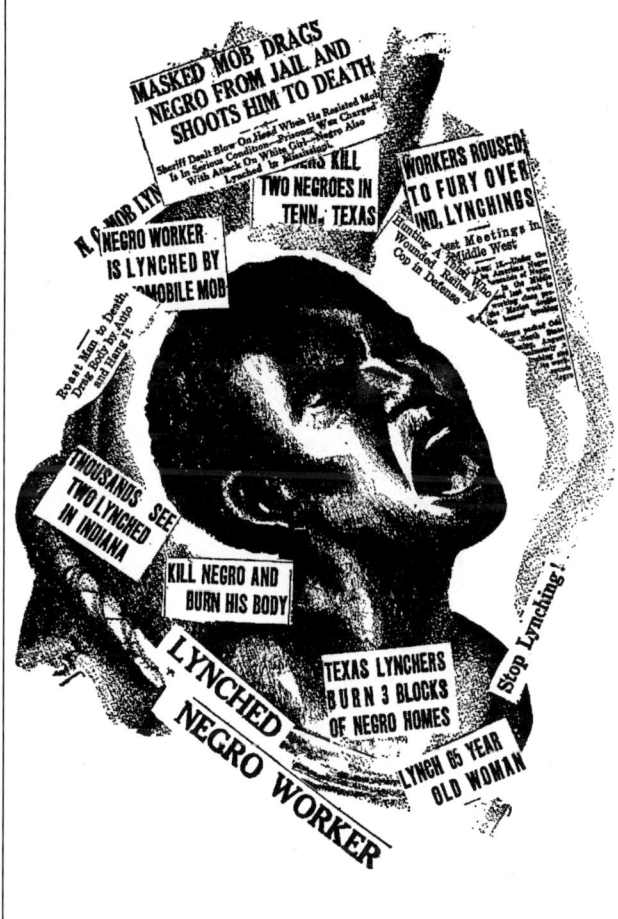

SOURCE 2 Extract from a magazine article, 'The Riot in Harlem' by Hamilton Basso in *New Republic*, April 3, 1935

" Relief has been inadequate. Charges have been made that it is one-third lower in Harlem than elsewhere. Some unemployed Negroes say they have to wait days, and some say weeks, before getting assistance. Relief administration has been entirely in the hands of white persons. "

SOURCE 3 Sean Dennis Cashman, *America in the Twenties and the Thirties*, 1989

" Black sociologist Kelly Miller described the black American in 1932 as the 'surplus man, the last to be hired and the first to be fired.' By 1933, 50 per cent of urban blacks could not find jobs of any kind ... unemployed whites contested for menial work they would have thought beneath them and thus 'negro jobs' disappeared as domestic service and garbage collection became white occupations ... [while in the South] Not only did the southern states provide the lowest levels of unemployment benefit and relief but white officials openly discriminated against blacks ... In Mississippi, where over half the population was black, less than 9 per cent of Afro-Americans received any relief in 1932, compared with 14 per cent of whites. "

1. In what ways do these sources show how the Depression was worse for blacks?

WORKSHEET 26
Why did Roosevelt win the 1932 election?

Give a set of cards, cut up and jumbled up, to each pair or group of students.

- Roosevelt and the Democrats had positive policies for dealing with the Depression.

- He promised direct action, for example, more relief from Federal Government to help those in need, schemes for unemployed young people.

- He promised a New Deal: to get industry back on its feet and get people back into jobs; also to create a fairer society.

- He promised to end Prohibition and the social evils it had created.

- Roosevelt's personality and the way he conducted his campaign persuaded people to vote for him.

- His determination had helped him overcome polio and personal difficulties, so Americans felt he could help them overcome their problems.

- He was a very good speaker and had a warm and friendly manner.

- Americans felt they could trust him.

- He travelled thousands of miles over America on his campaign to meet millions of people. Americans felt he cared about them.

- Hoover was very unpopular. He seemed to be cold and distant. He appeared not to care about what was happening to thousands of suffering Americans.

- He seemed to think that the Depression was just a blip, that prosperity was just around the corner.

- People disliked him for his shameful treatment of the Bonus Marchers.

- Republican policies had not been acceptable to the American people.

- Many Americans felt that their policies did not do enough to help find a way out of the Depression, to provide relief and more jobs.

- The Republicans relied on business to get the USA out of the Depression but the American people no longer trusted business.

- The Republicans seemed determined to carry on Prohibition.

WORKSHEET 27
The New Deal in action

Decide whether the agencies and acts below were concerned with relief, recovery or reform and put a tick in the appropriate column. Remember that some agencies served more than one purpose. In the final column explain what the agency did.

Agency	Relief	Recovery	Reform	In what ways did the agency provide relief, help recovery or bring reform
FERA				
HOLC				
CCC				
CWA				
PWA				
AAA				
NRA				
TVA				
WPA				
RA/FSA				
Wagner Act				
Social Security Act				

© JOHN MURRAY *The USA between the Wars Teachers' Resource Book*

WORKSHEET 28

Criticising the New Deal

Use the ideas below to help you write the letter to a newspaper from a rich Republican business person.

Editor
New York Times
November 16, 1936

Dear Editor,

It's time all right-thinking people got together to restrain this mad man in the White House. The New Deal is not only damaging the American economy, it is ruining the very spirit that made this country great …

The New Deal is wasteful …

The amount of tax we have to pay is unfair …

Businesses have been damaged because of:
– too many regulations
– social security payments
– unions

Roosevelt is acting like a dictator …

The New Deal is damaging the 'self-reliance' of Americans …

You could end your letter by putting in a last sentence condemning Roosevelt.

WORKSHEET 29

Opponents of the New Deal

Use the charts below to record the main points made by the people opposing the New Deal.

	Objections to New Deal
Republicans	
Business	
Rich	

	Objections to New Deal and alternative ideas to help people
Huey Long	
Francis Townsend	
Father Coughlin	

WORKSHEET 30
Assessing the New Deal

Use this grid to help you think about how successful the New Deal was. See page 122 in your textbook.

Aim	Success			Failure	
	+2	+1	0	-1	-2
Bring government 'action, and action now'					
Put people back to work					
Restore confidence in banks					
Stop more businesses collapsing					
Help the poor					
Increase wages of people in work					
Restore farmers' income					
Help the Tennessee Valley and stop further soil erosion					
Help all Americans					
Restore Americans' faith in themselves					
Improve relations between bosses and workers					
Revive the American economy					
Make America a better place for ordinary people					

The USA between the Wars   Teachers' Resource Book   © JOHN MURRAY

WORKSHEET 31

Two views of the NRA

The New Deal introduced a vast number of measures in a short space of time. It was unlikely that all of them would work perfectly. This example looks at different views about the way the National Recovery Administration worked.

> **SOURCE 1** John Spivak, a radical critic of the New Deal, thought the NRA helped businesses rather than workers. He recorded this conversation with a young woman working in a North Carolina cotton mill
>
> " 'How're things?' I asked …
> 'All right,' she said, swiftly.
> 'Better since the NRA?'
> 'Yeah.'
> 'How much do you make?'
> 'Twelve-fifty.'
> 'How many hours?'
> 'Eight. We used to work twelve.'
> 'Less hours and more pay, eh? NRA do that?'
> 'Yeah. But we got doubled-up.'
> 'What's that?'
> 'Doubled-up. Stretched-out. We got to do twice as much work as we used to. Got to work faster too. So it's all the same as before. We get exactly what we got before.'
> 'How much was that?'
> 'Six dollars a week. Now we work twice as much so we get twelve dollars. No difference.'
> 'But you have four hours extra a day, haven't you?'
> 'Yeah. But what good's that? I'm too tired to go out when I get through.'
> Everywhere, throughout the country, I heard the same cry from the workers: the speed-up, the killing speed-up which is exhausting their bodies sending them home sodden and spent, with just energy to eat and rest for the next day's grind. "

1. How are these two accounts different?

> **SOURCE 2** Frances Perkins, Secretary of Labour in Roosevelt's cabinet, in a 1934 book defending the New Deal, also recorded an interview with a cotton-mill worker
>
> " A cotton mill worker in North Carolina says: 'I think the NRA is a great thing. It has put more money in my pay and the short hours has made a new person out of me, as when I worked 11 hours I could not feel like going anywhere to have a good time. Now I have plenty of time for rest and play. I hope there will always be an NRA. "

2. How can you account for this difference if both are personal testimony which is not made up? Do you think it is to do with:
- the attitudes of the women workers themselves
- different conditions in the factories where they worked
- the views of the people who wrote the accounts
- a combination of the above?

3. Do you think one of the the sources is more reliable than the other? Explain your answer.

WORKSHEET 32

How successful was the New Deal?

Give a set of cards, cut up and jumbled up to each pair or group of students.

The New Deal did not bring full economic recovery.	The number of unemployed remained high throughout the 1930s. The level of production did not rise significantly until the war.	When the government stopped paying out lots of money, unemployment went up. This meant that businesses had not recovered sufficiently to keep going without government help.
Only the demand from other countries and from the US armed forces in the Second World War drove up the demand for goods, got production going and people back into work.	The New Deal did help the economy and businesses.	The banking reforms during the first Hundred Days helped to stop further financial collapse. Many more businesses might have collapsed if more banks had failed.
Loans were made to businesses to help them survive.	The New Deal put confidence back into Americans to start buying goods again.	The New Deal helped farmers and workers in trade unions.
The AAA had substantially increased farmers' incomes by 1937.	Loans were given to farmers so that they did not lose their farms.	Government support in the NRA and the Wagner Act forced employers to recognise trade unions and helped workers to negotiate higher wages.

WORKSHEET 32 (continued)

The New Deal helped a lot of people get through the Depression.	Enormous amounts of money were made available to provide relief to help people survive, help them meet basic needs and prevent them losing their homes.	Thousands of young men were taken by the CCC out in the countryside to get fit and healthy and do useful work.
Millions of dollars were spent on providing jobs in the WPA and PWA. This helped people earn some money and keep their self-respect.	There were a number of groups that did not do well out of the New Deal.	Blacks were still segregated and discriminated against. They got the worst jobs and often their relief was not as high as that which whites received.
Women did not do particularly well, apart from a few women getting some important posts. The advances of the 1920s were held up for many.	Other minority groups got little out of the New Deal. These groups included Mexican-Americans and Puerto Ricans.	The New Deal produced results of lasting value.
Many hospitals, bridges, roads etc. were built through the public works programmes, e.g. the PWA and the WPA. A large part of the natural landscape was conserved.	The Tennessee Valley, which covered several states, was completely transformed. It gave a whole new lease of life to the area.	The New Deal created social welfare programmes, pensions and stronger labour unions which benefited Americans for many years.

WORKSHEET 33

An obituary for Franklin D. Roosevelt

Use the ideas below to help you with the Activity on page 125.

1. Decide whether you will write your obituary as a person supporting or attacking Roosevelt.
2. Write brief notes in each box as you collect evidence to support your statements about Roosevelt.

Early life

For: Born of famous political family, determined to overcome terrible illness
Against: Rich man from aristocratic family unlike self-made Republicans, e.g. Hoover

---

Getting elected as President

For: Brilliant campaign, offered people what they wanted
Against: People tricked by easy promises

Qualities as a leader

For: Special relationship with the people, inspired confidence
Against: Overbearing dictator

The New Deal

For: Wonderful achievement, helped millions of people get through Depression
Against: Waste of money, never brought recovery

Conclusions

For: Saved democracy, prevented extremism and violence, gave Americans hope
Against: Destroyed spirit of individualism and self-reliance that made America great